Utterly Adorable Animals

A Coloring Book for Kids and Adults

Comprised by Gabriel Llhewellyn-Ari

Published 2016

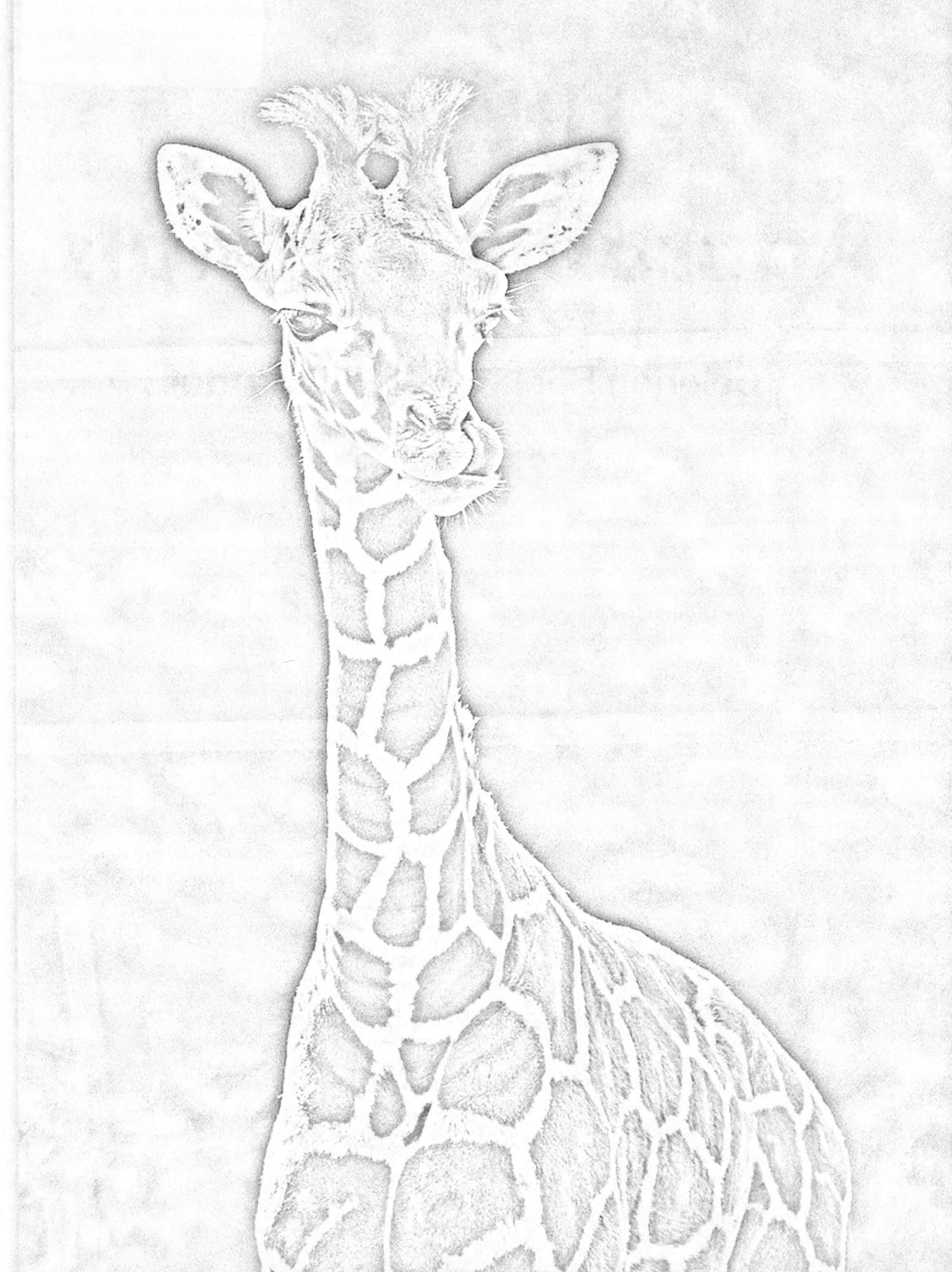

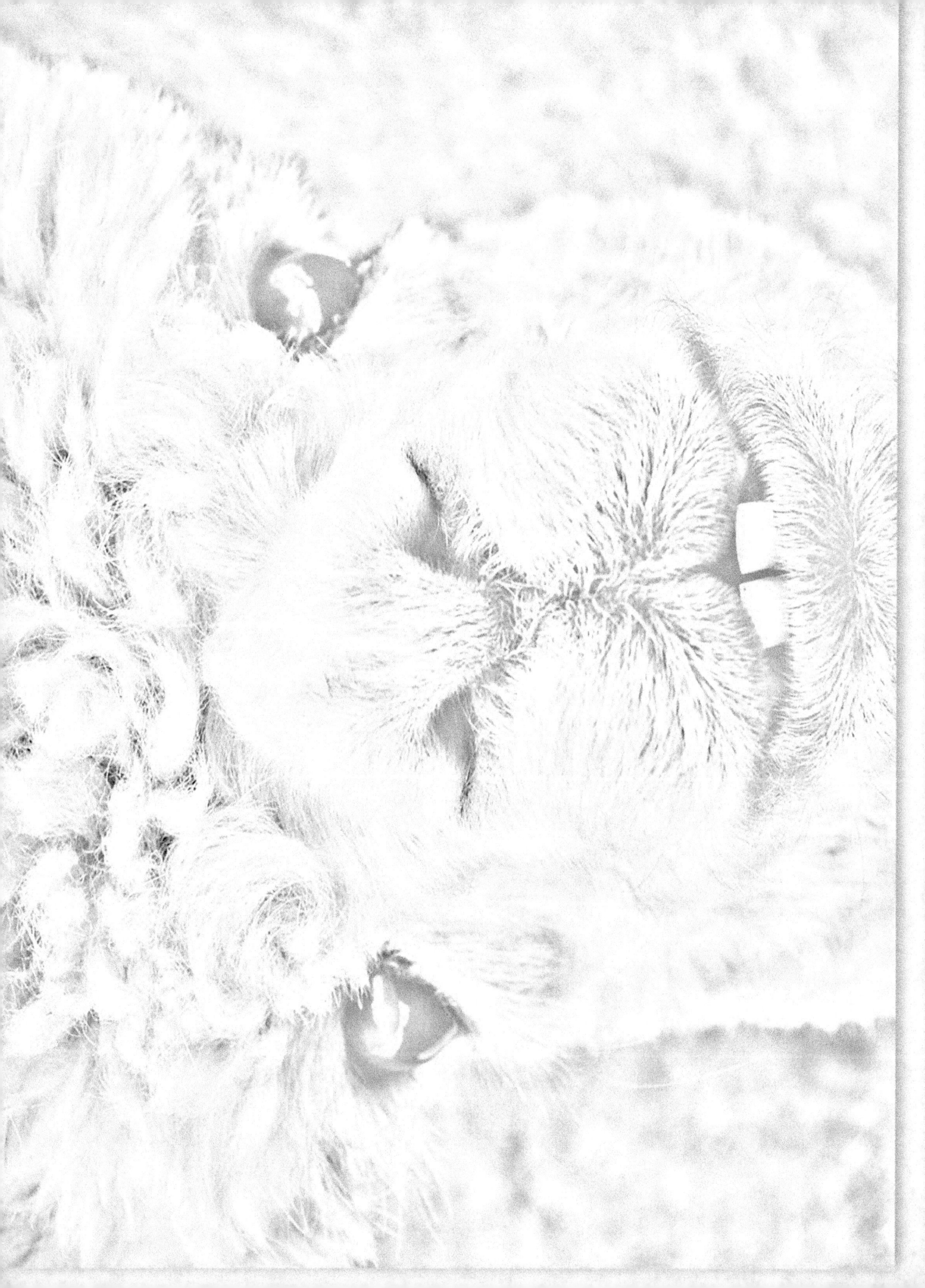

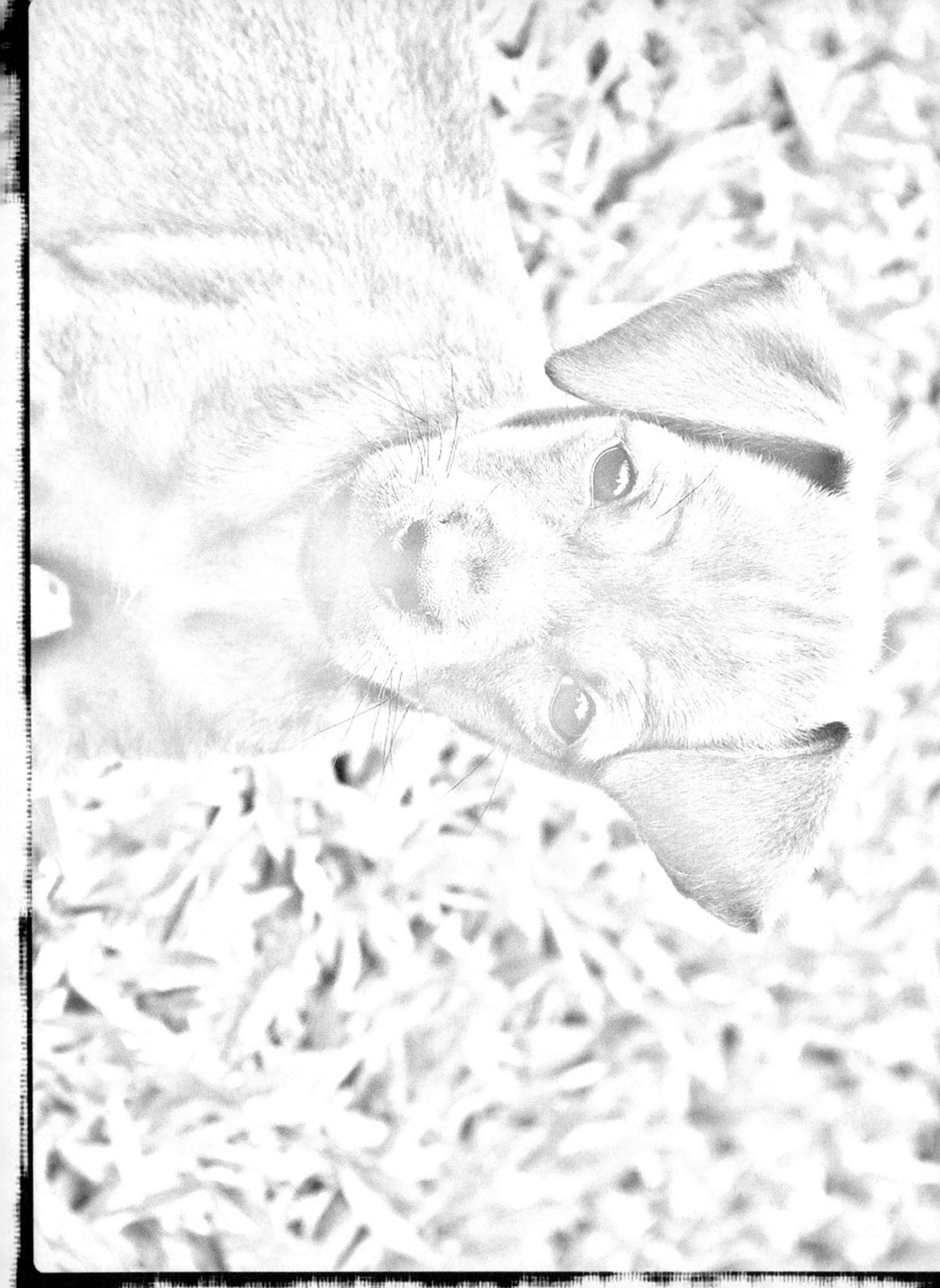

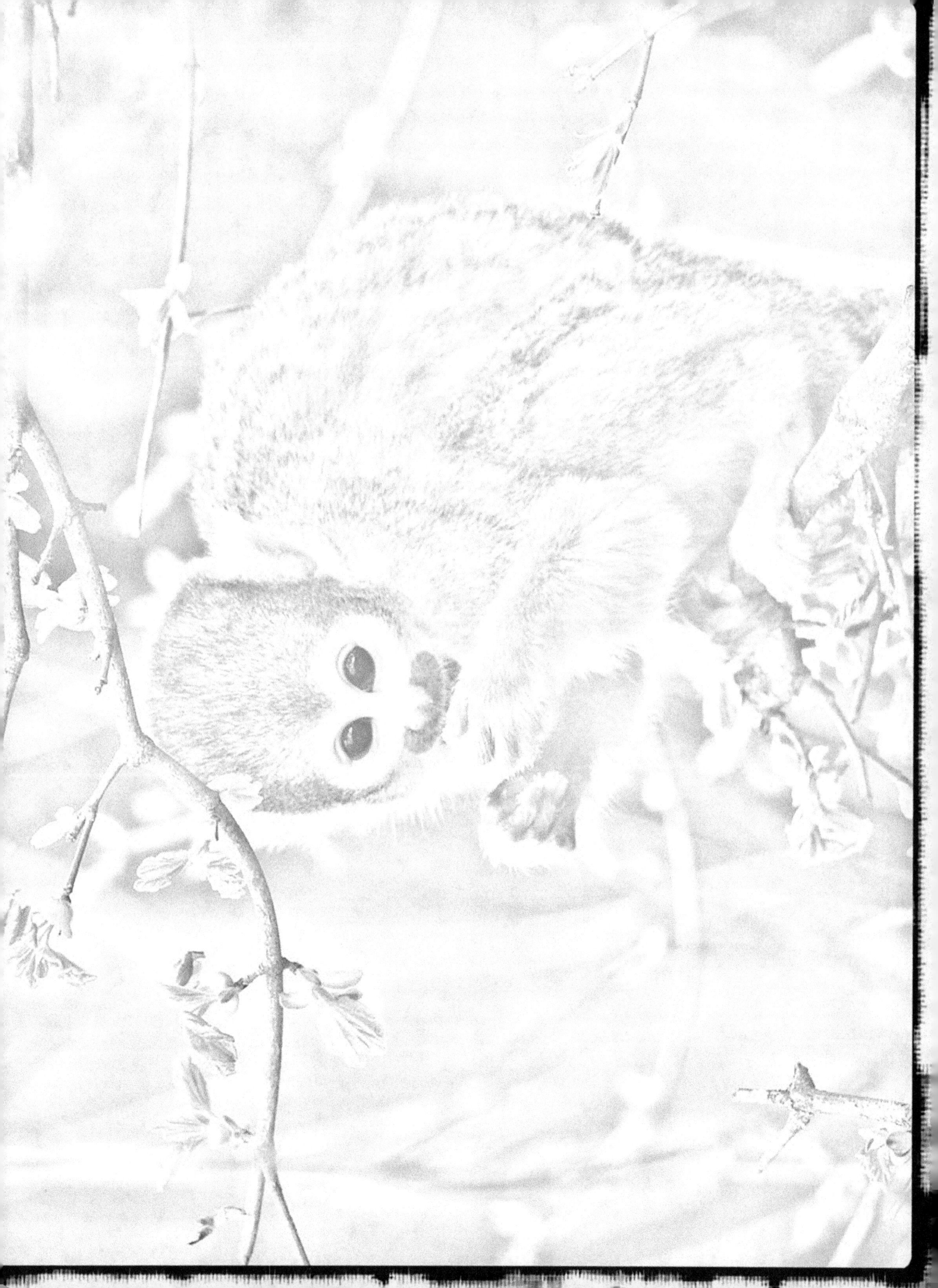

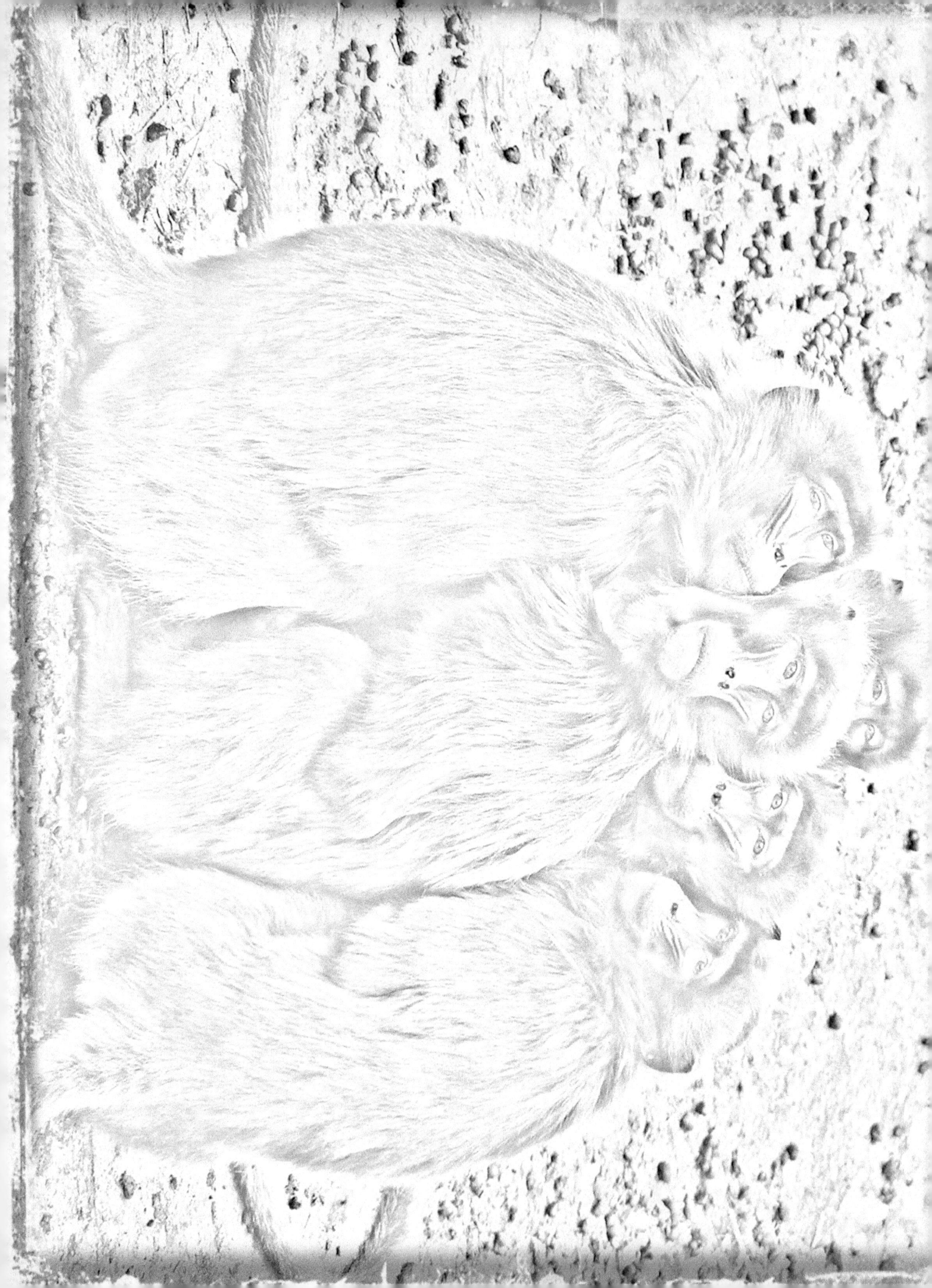

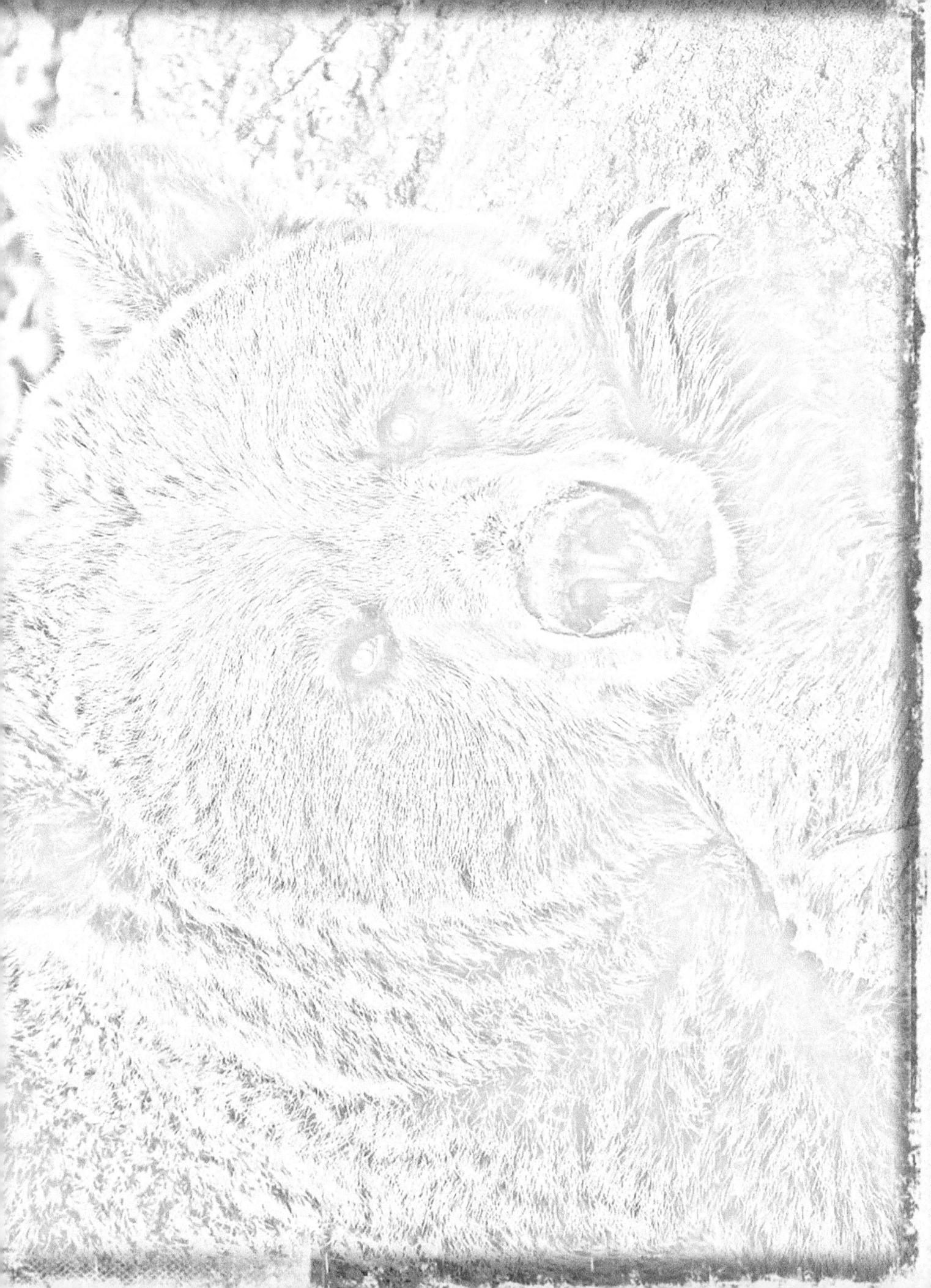

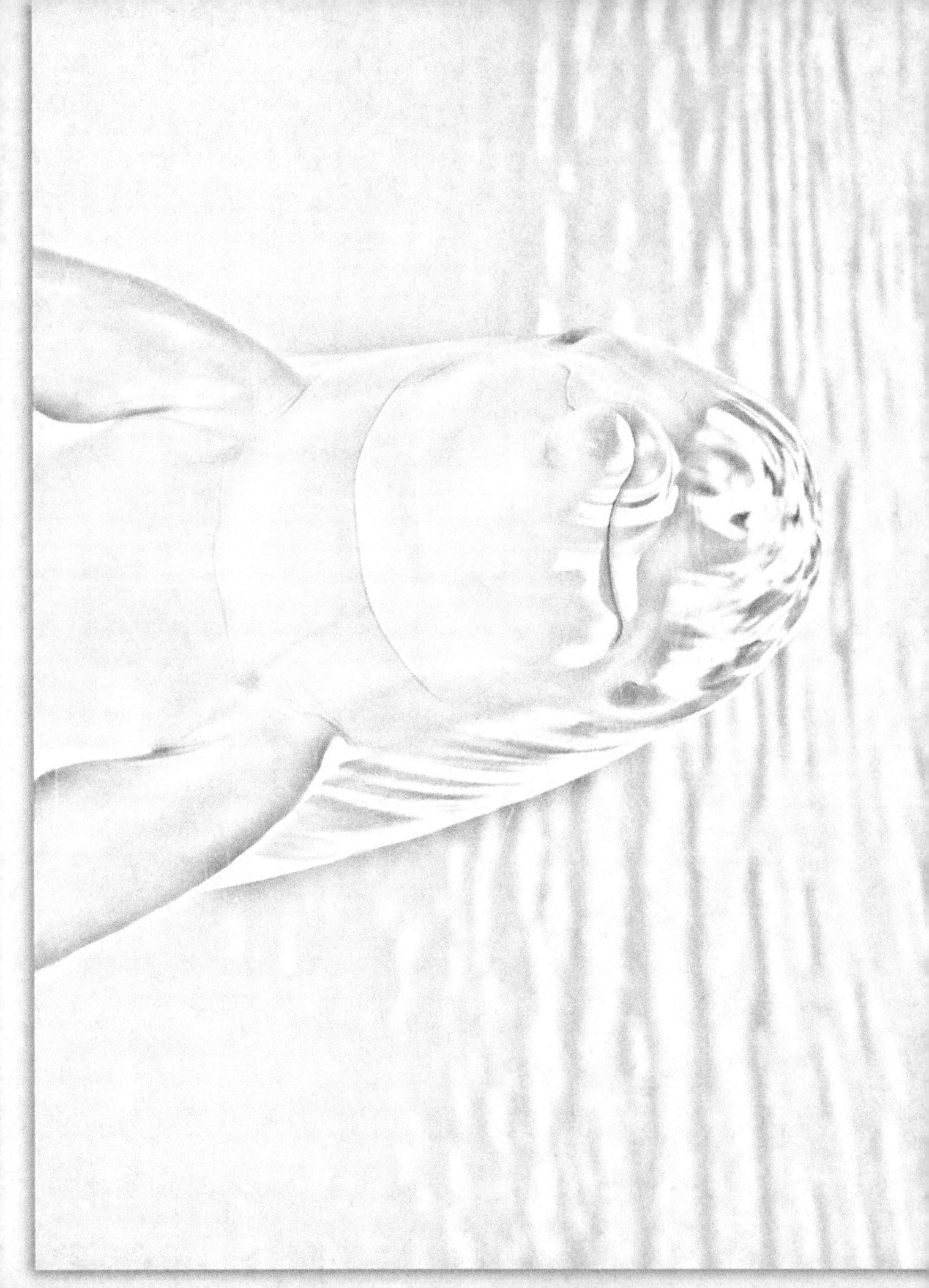

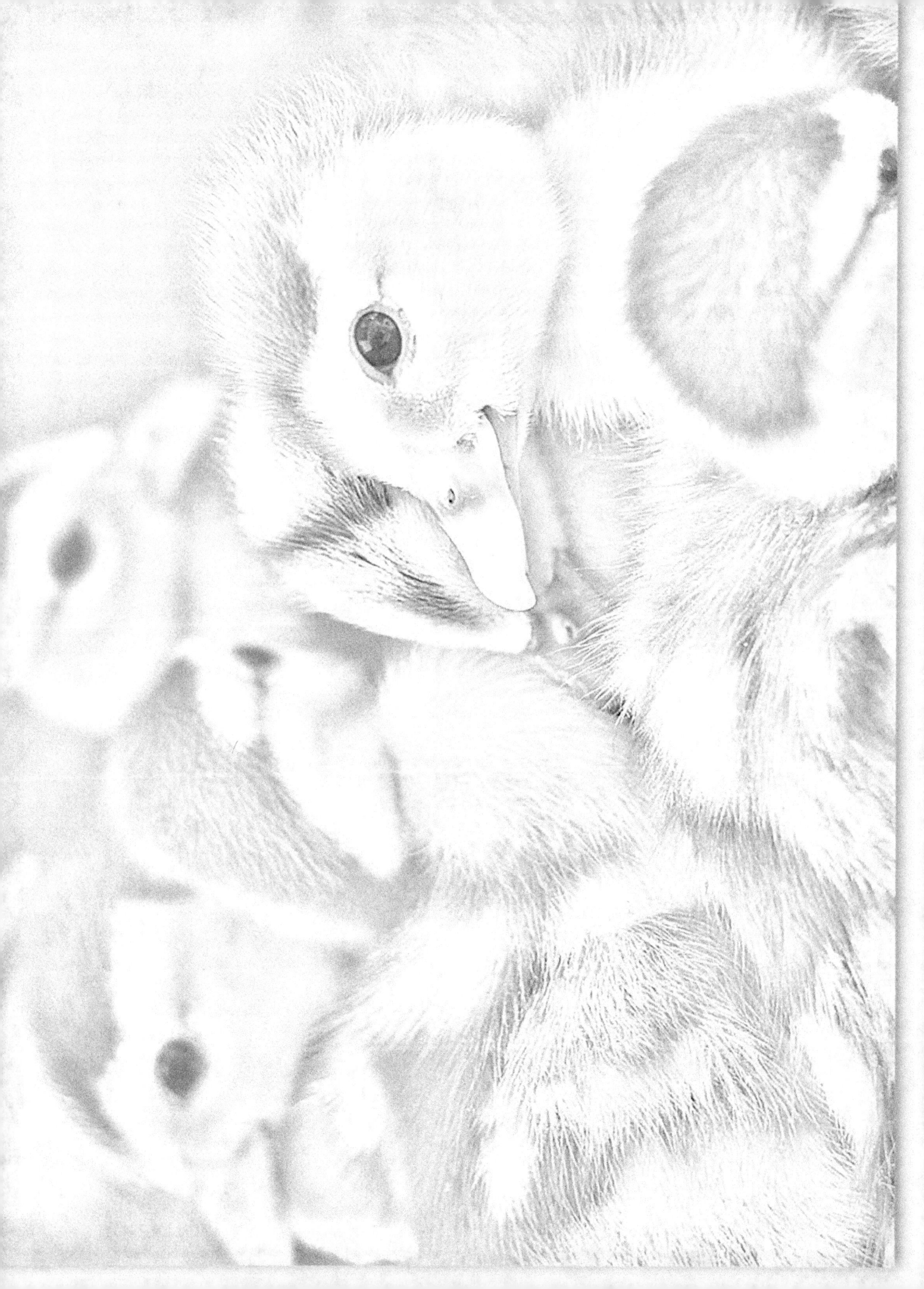

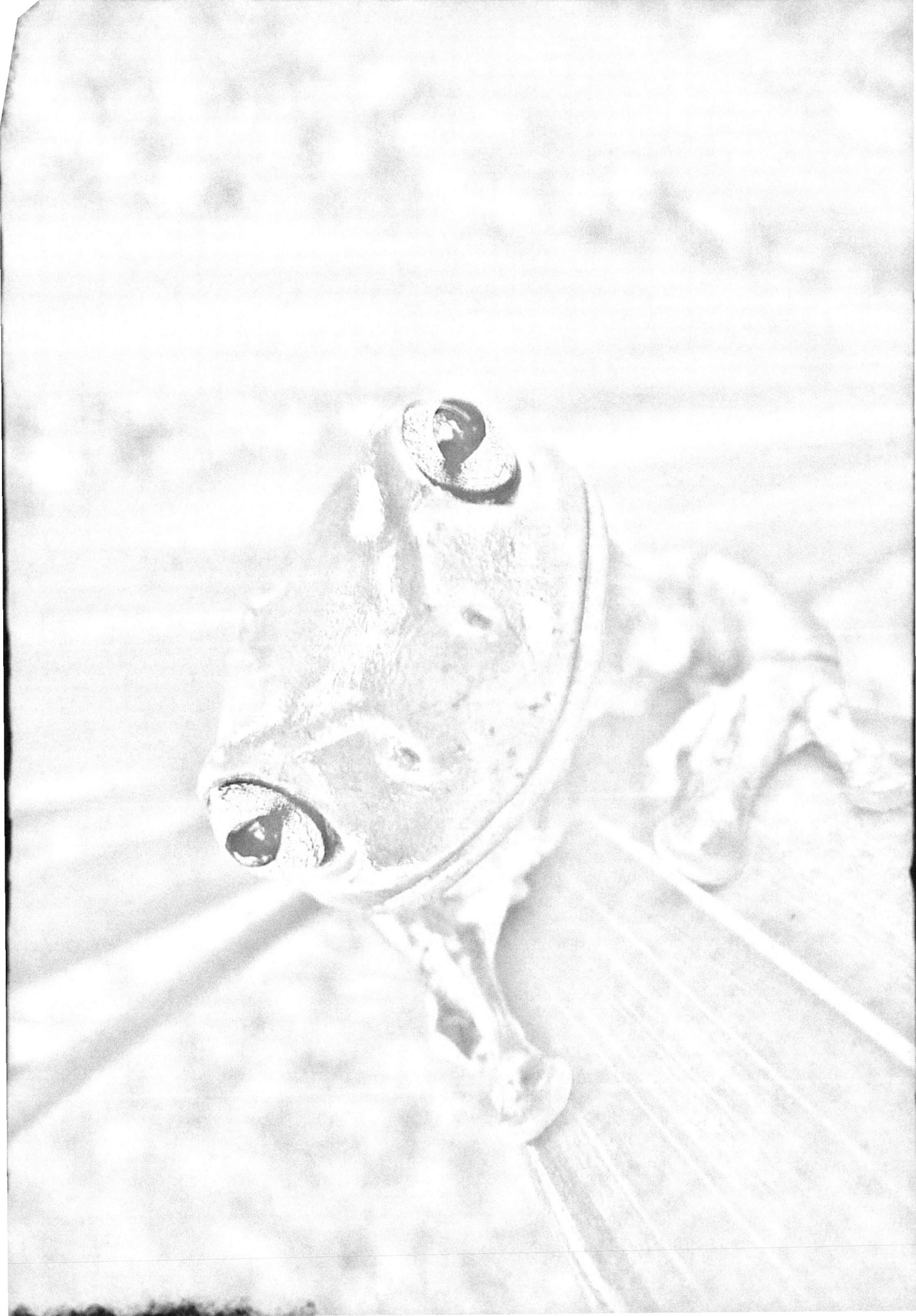

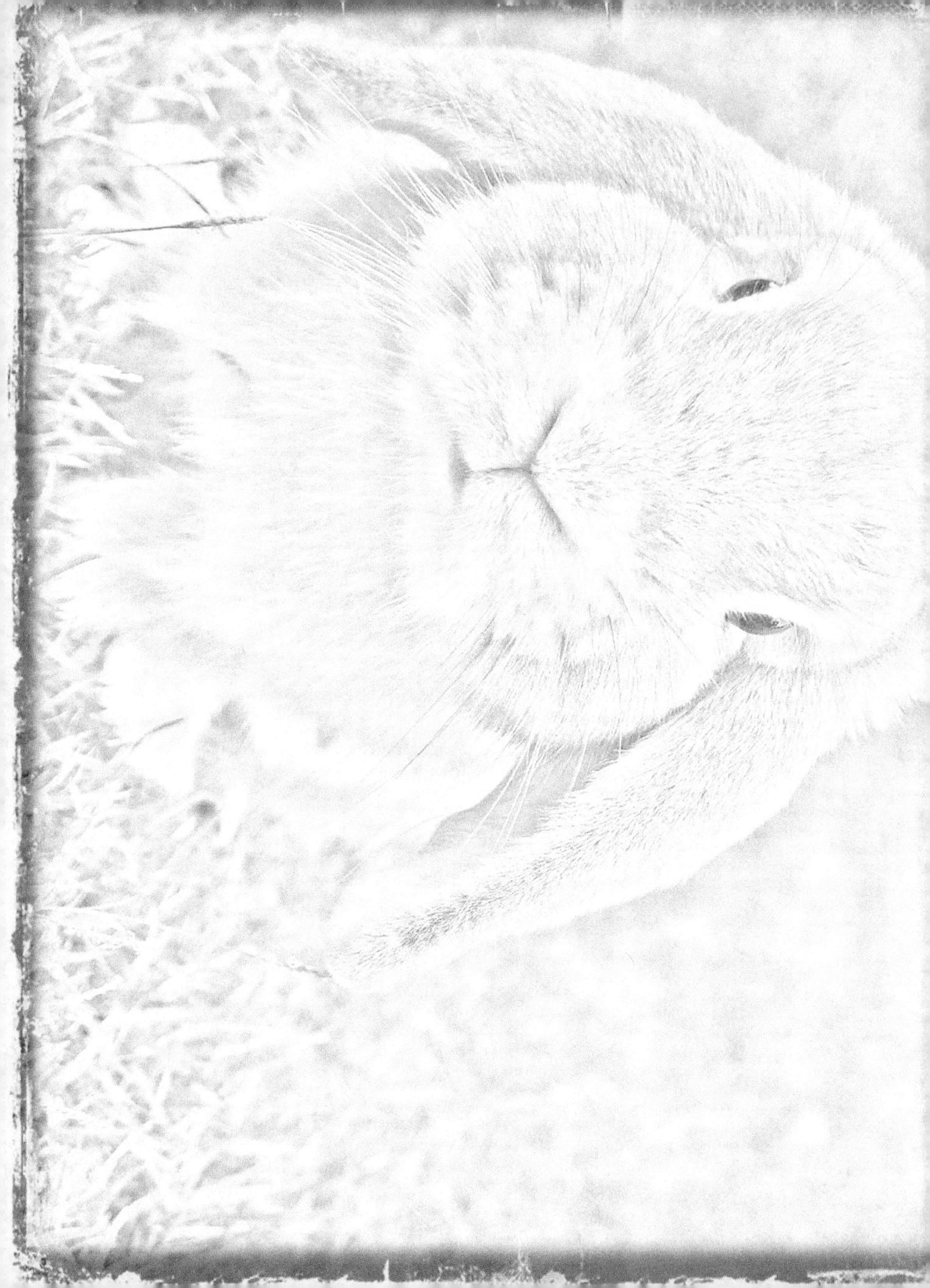

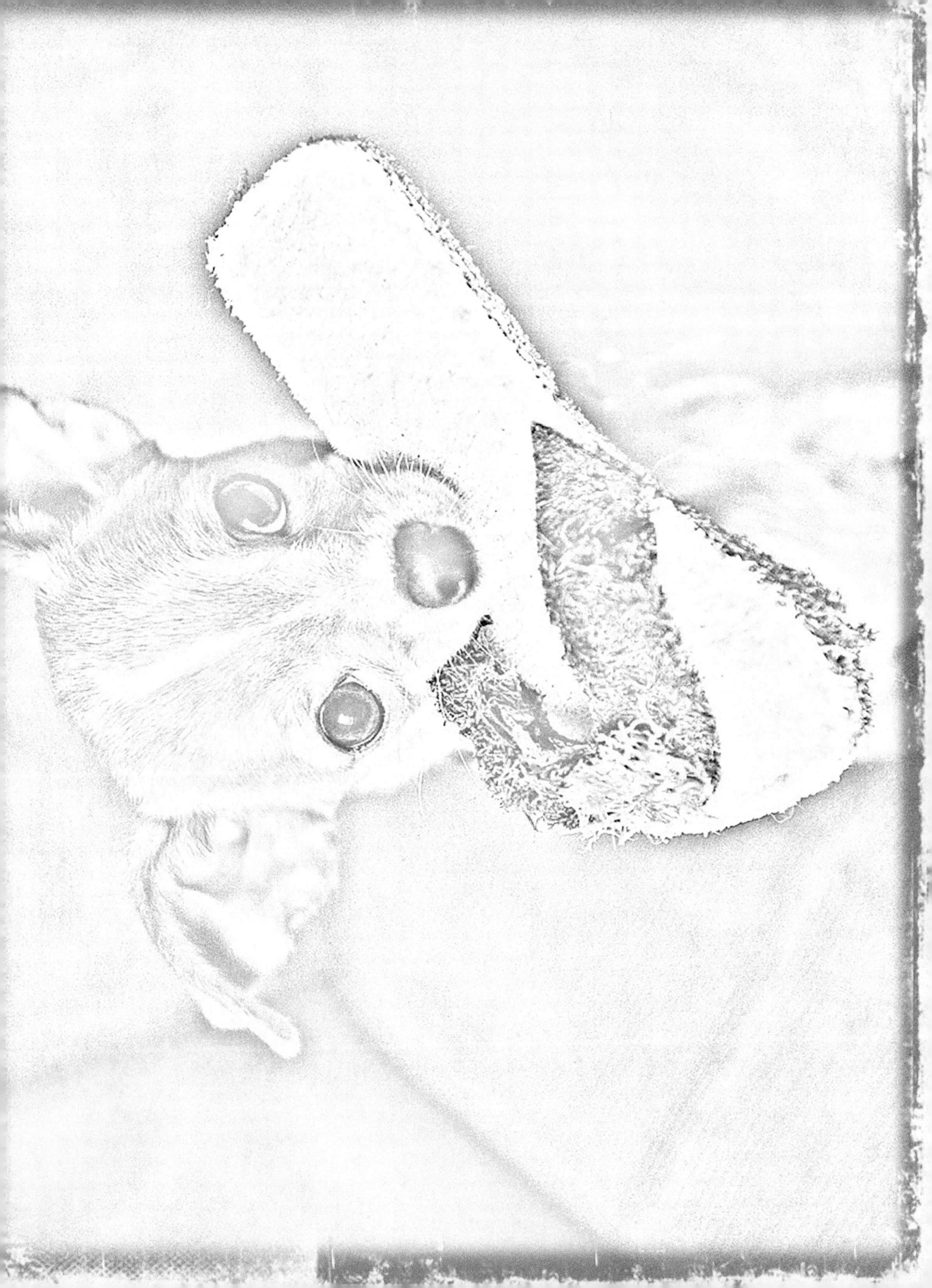

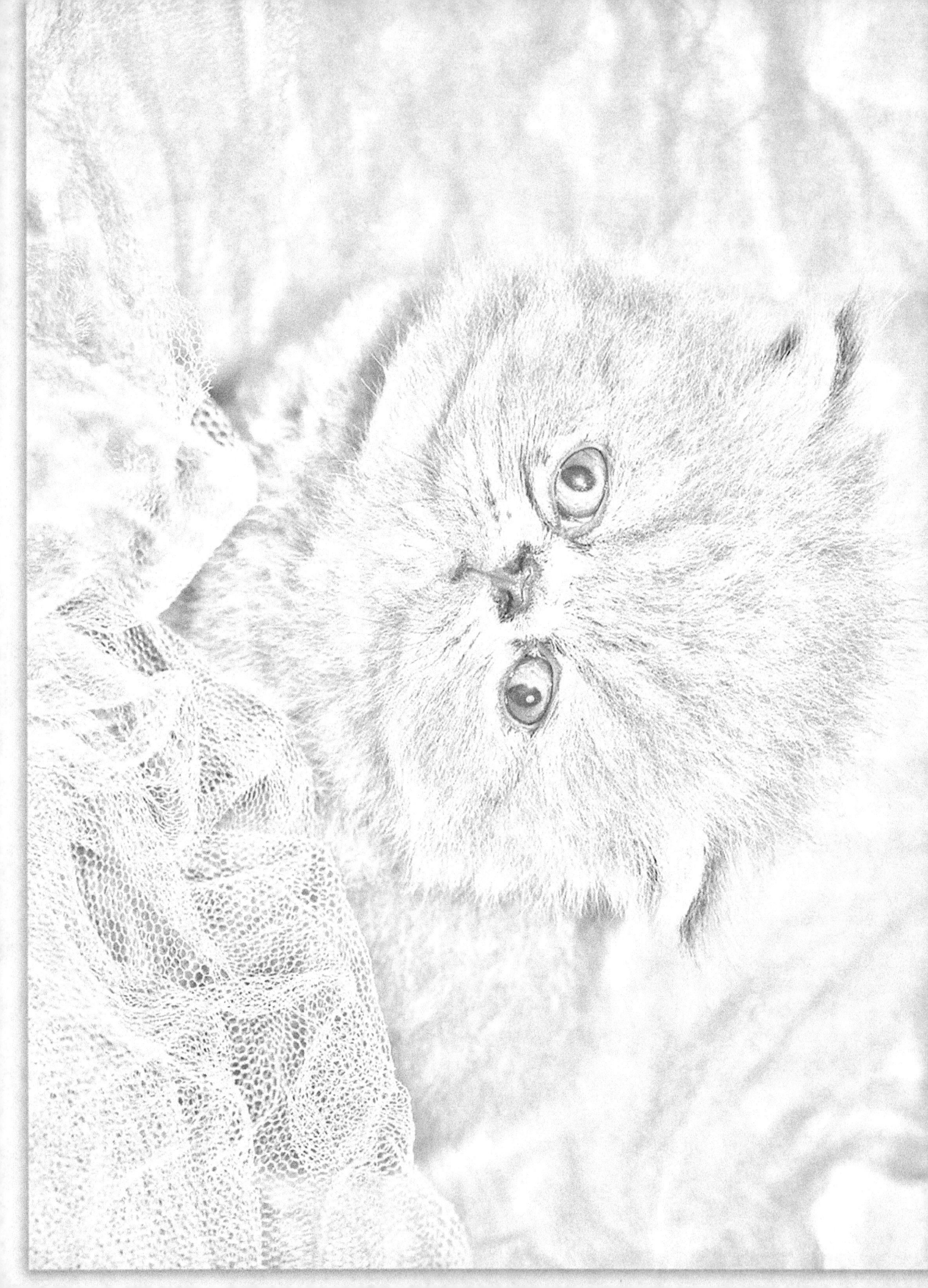

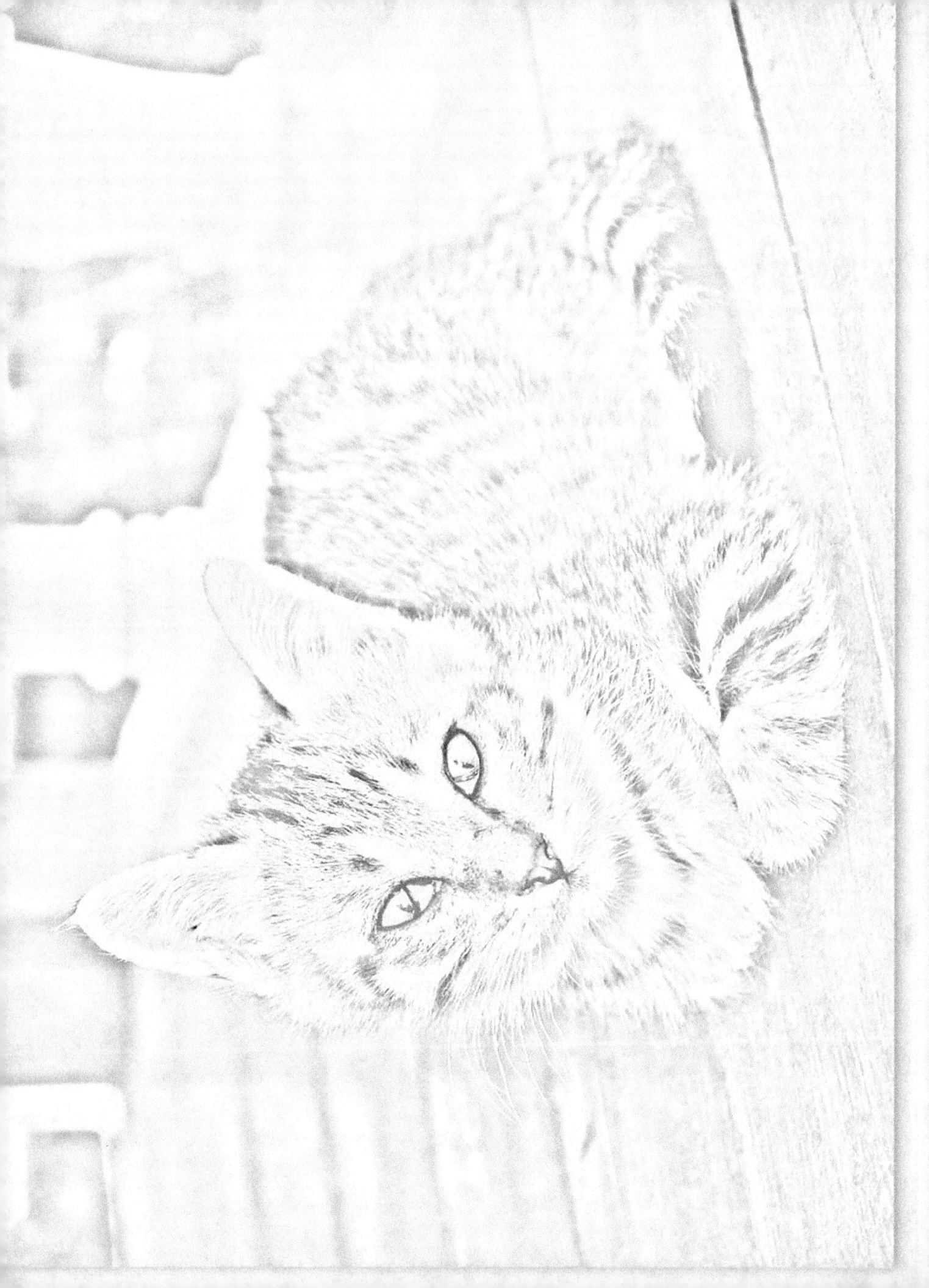

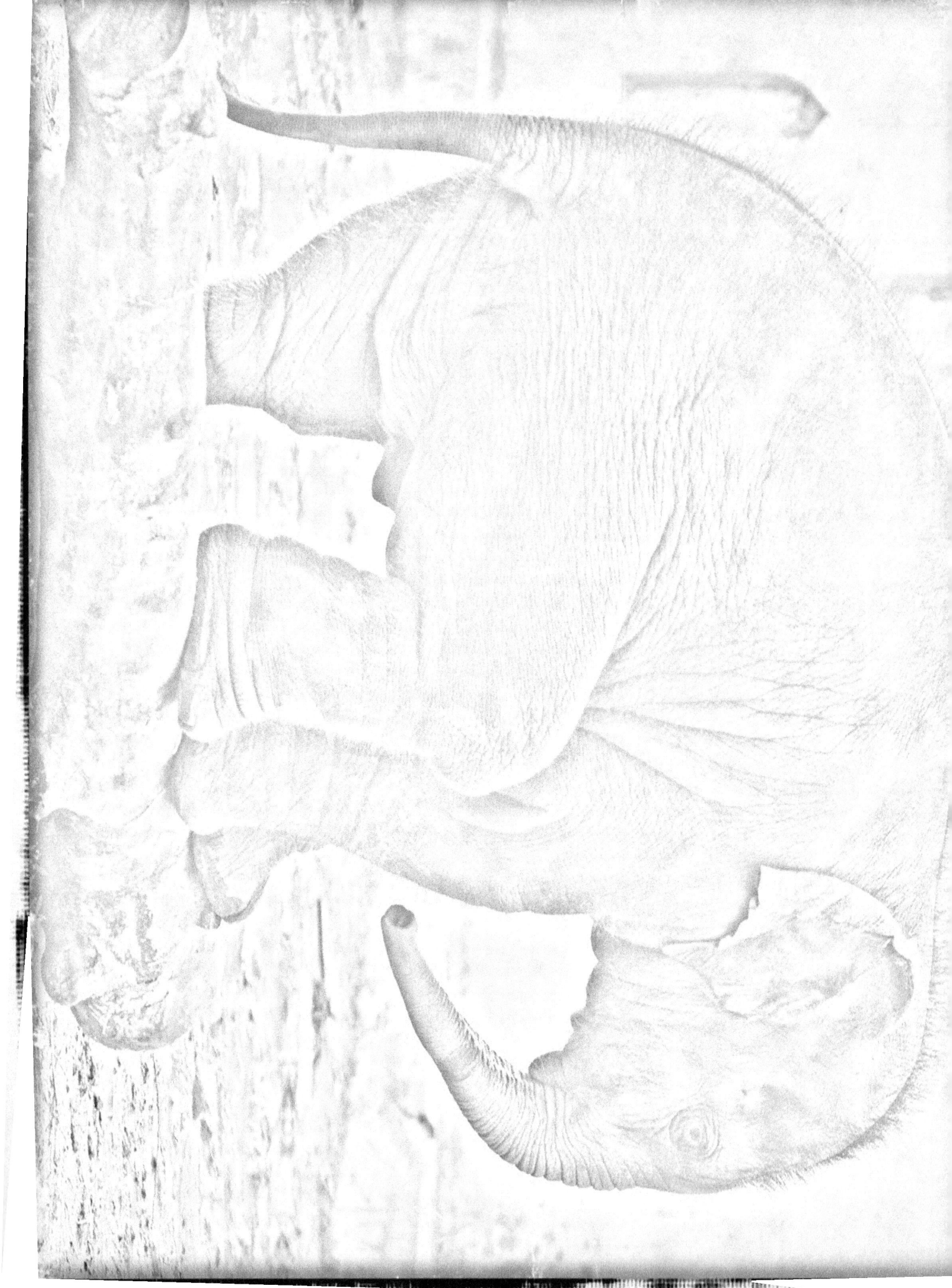

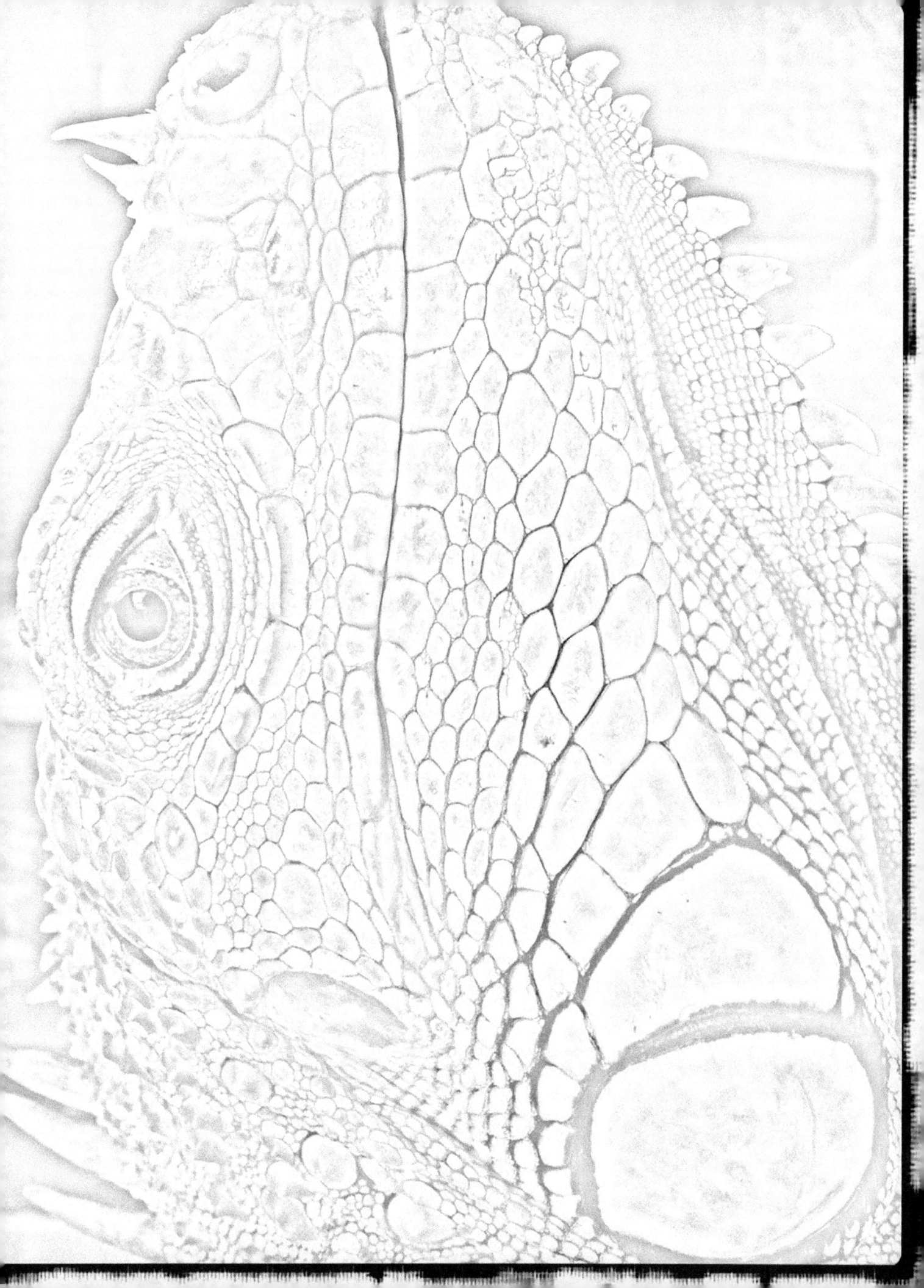

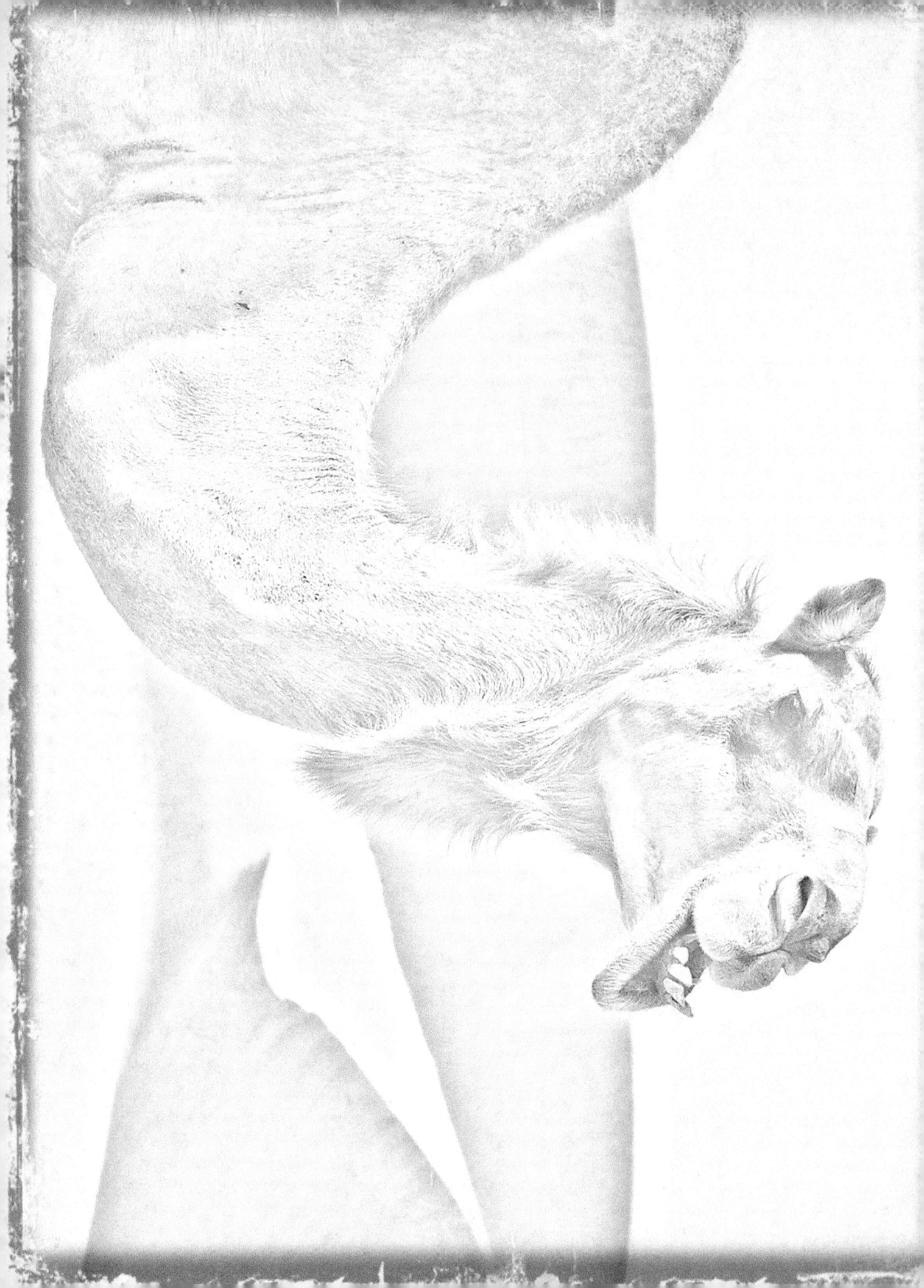

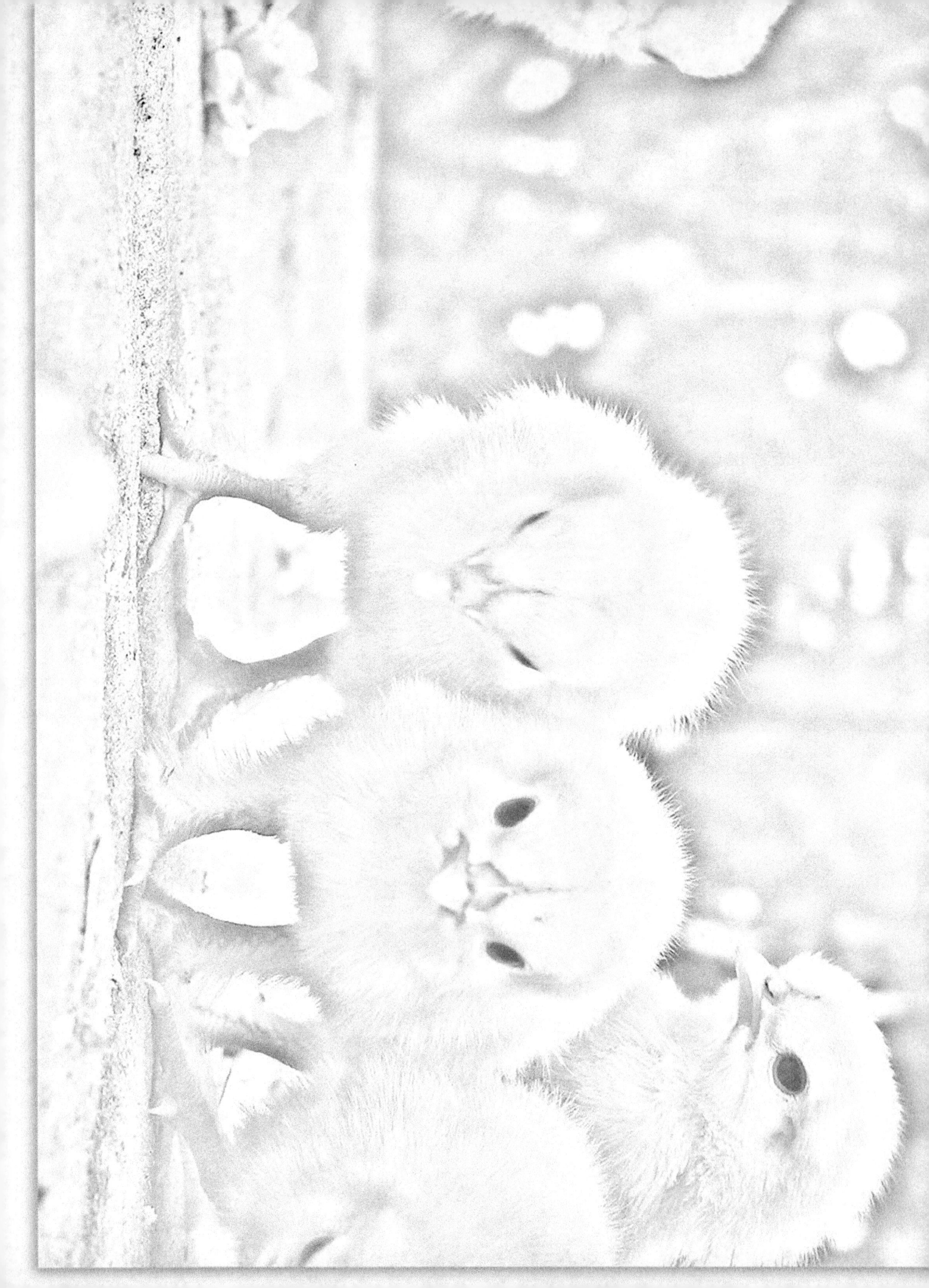

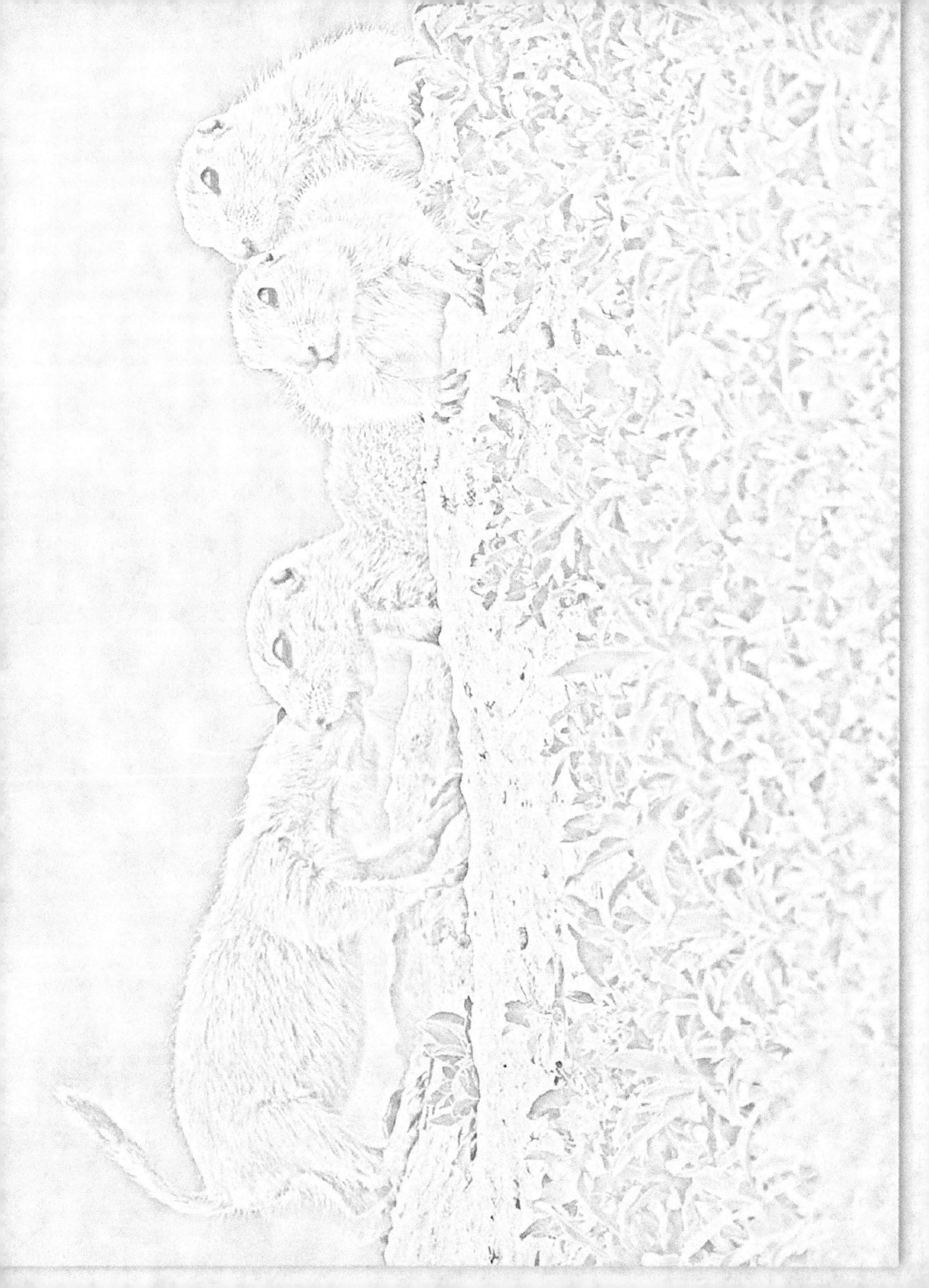

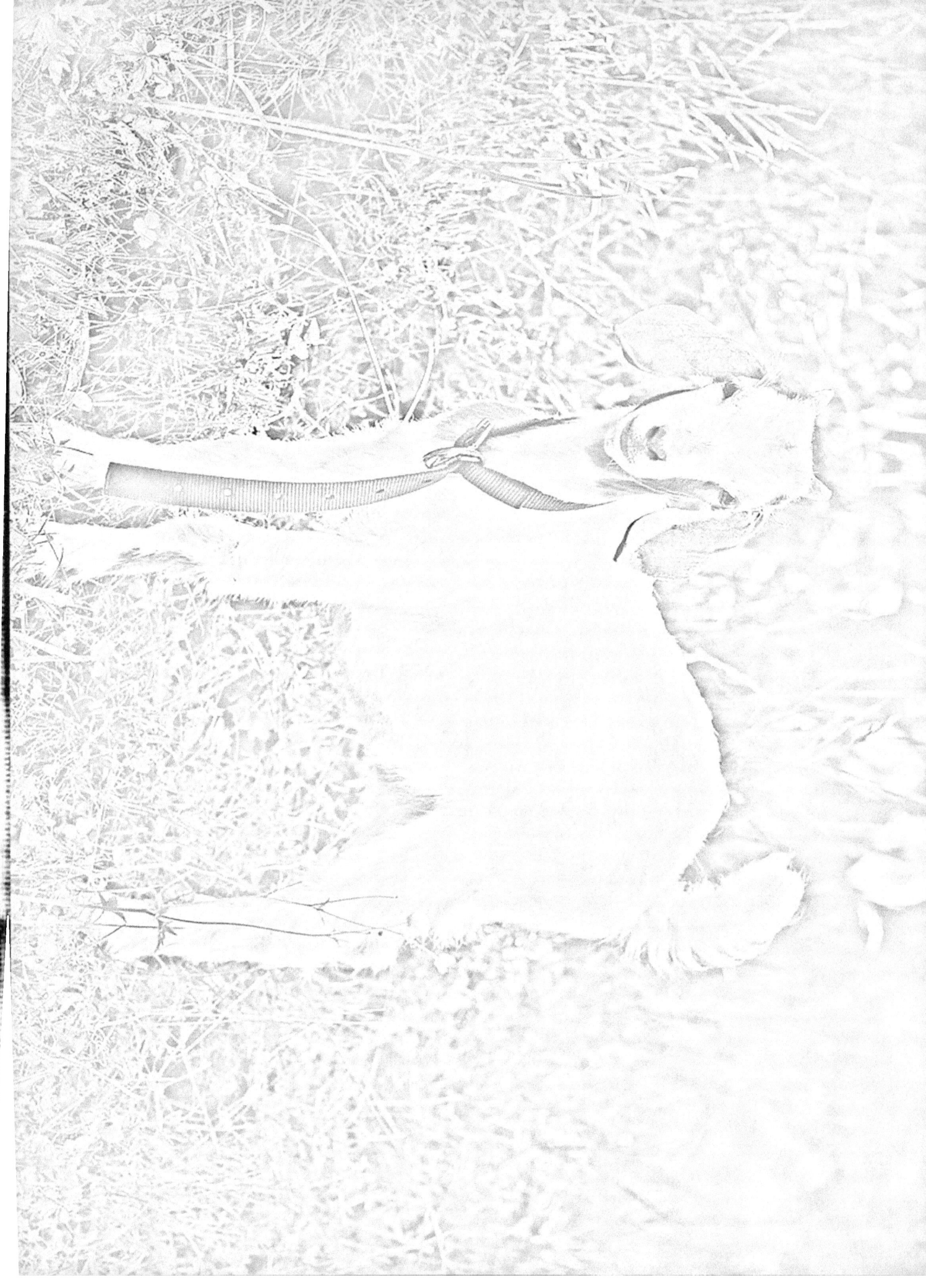

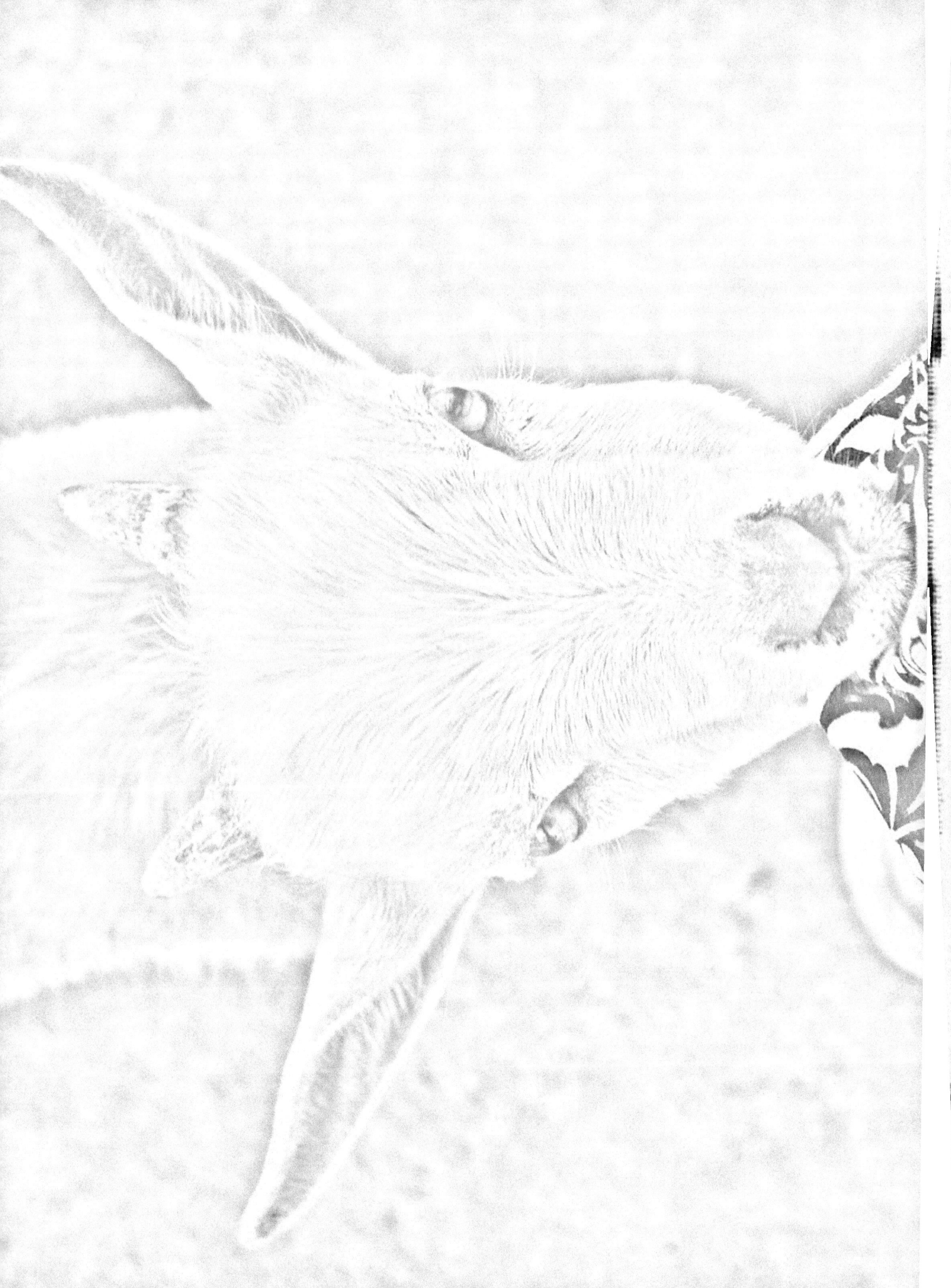

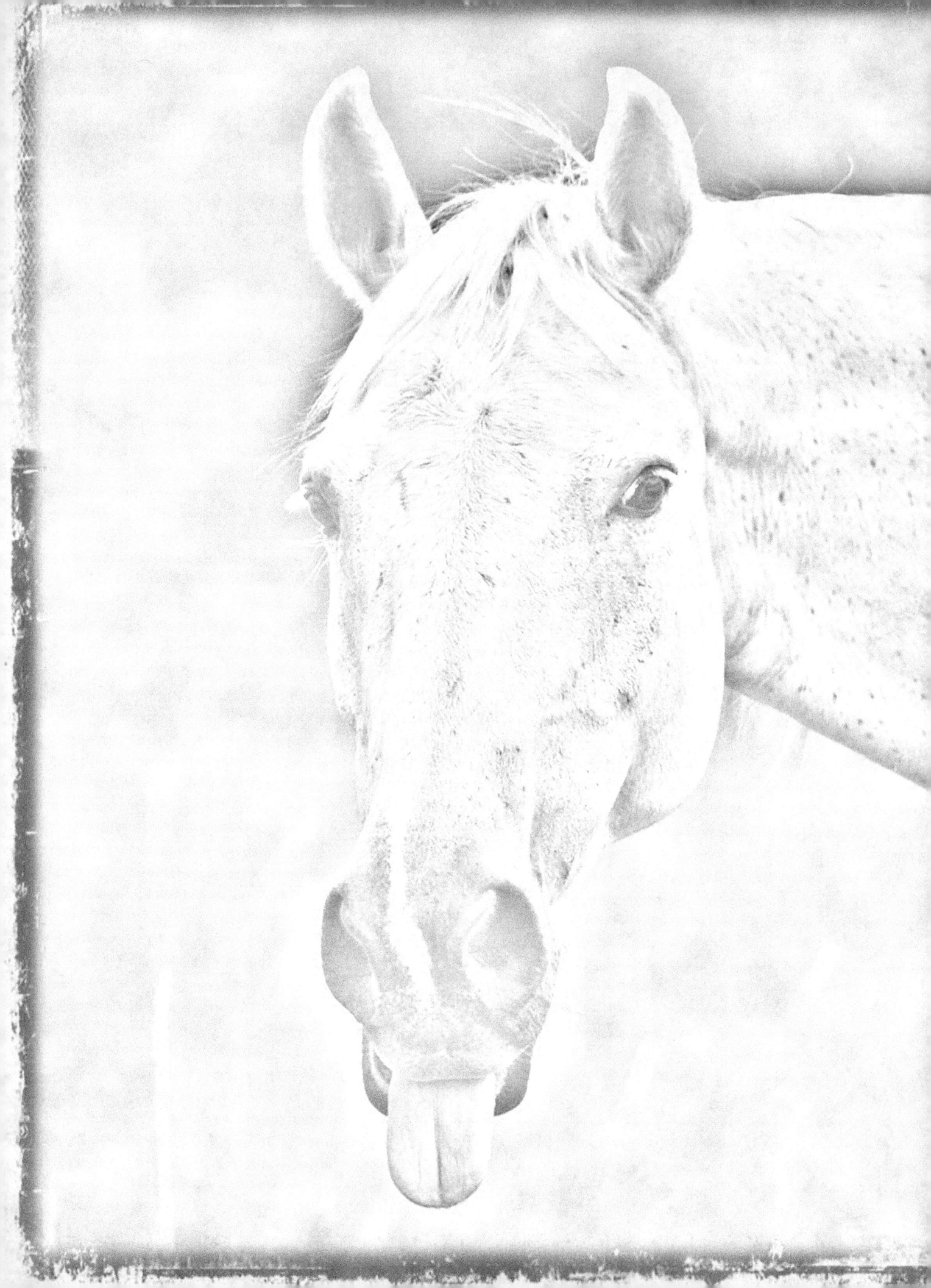

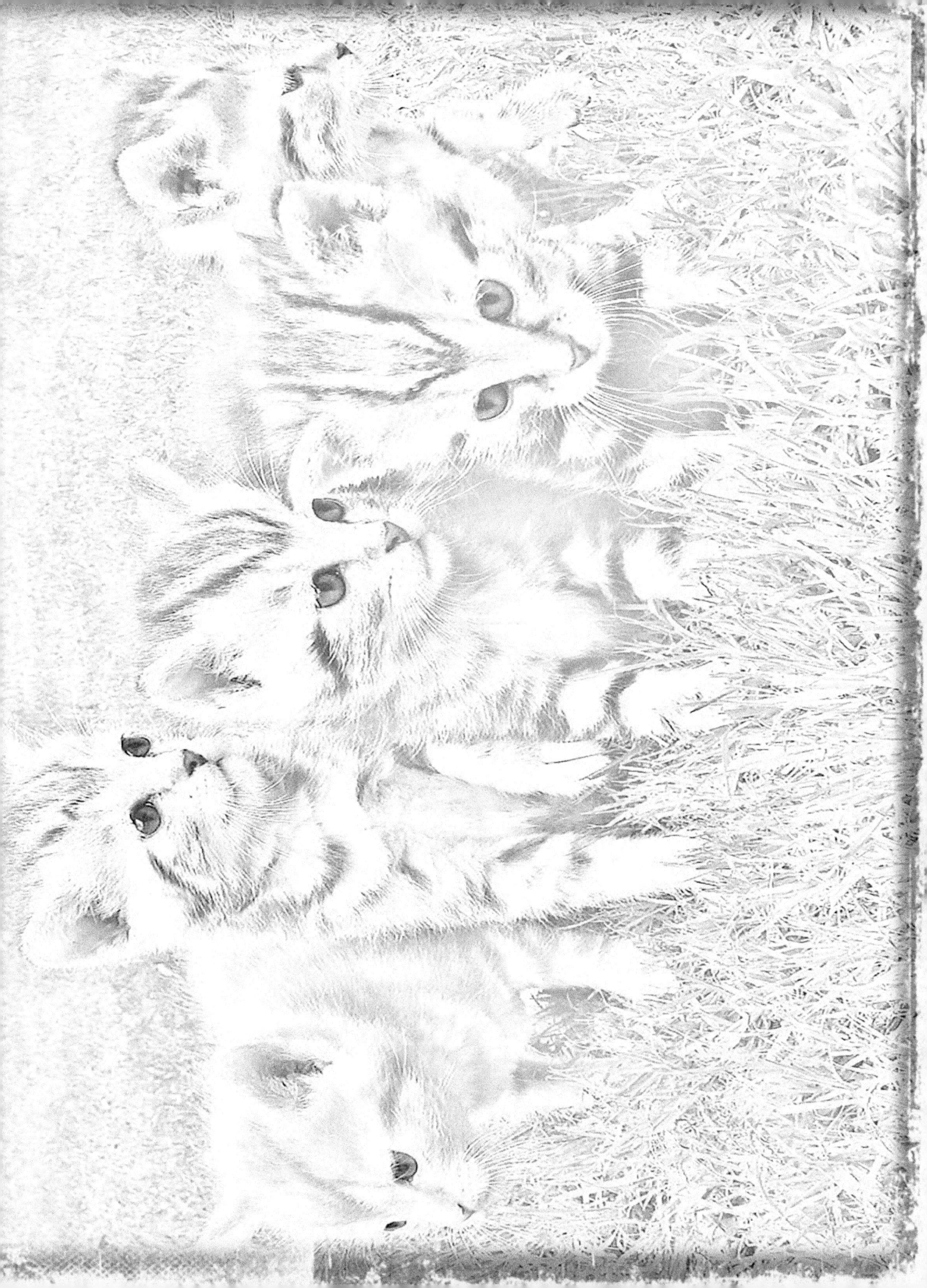

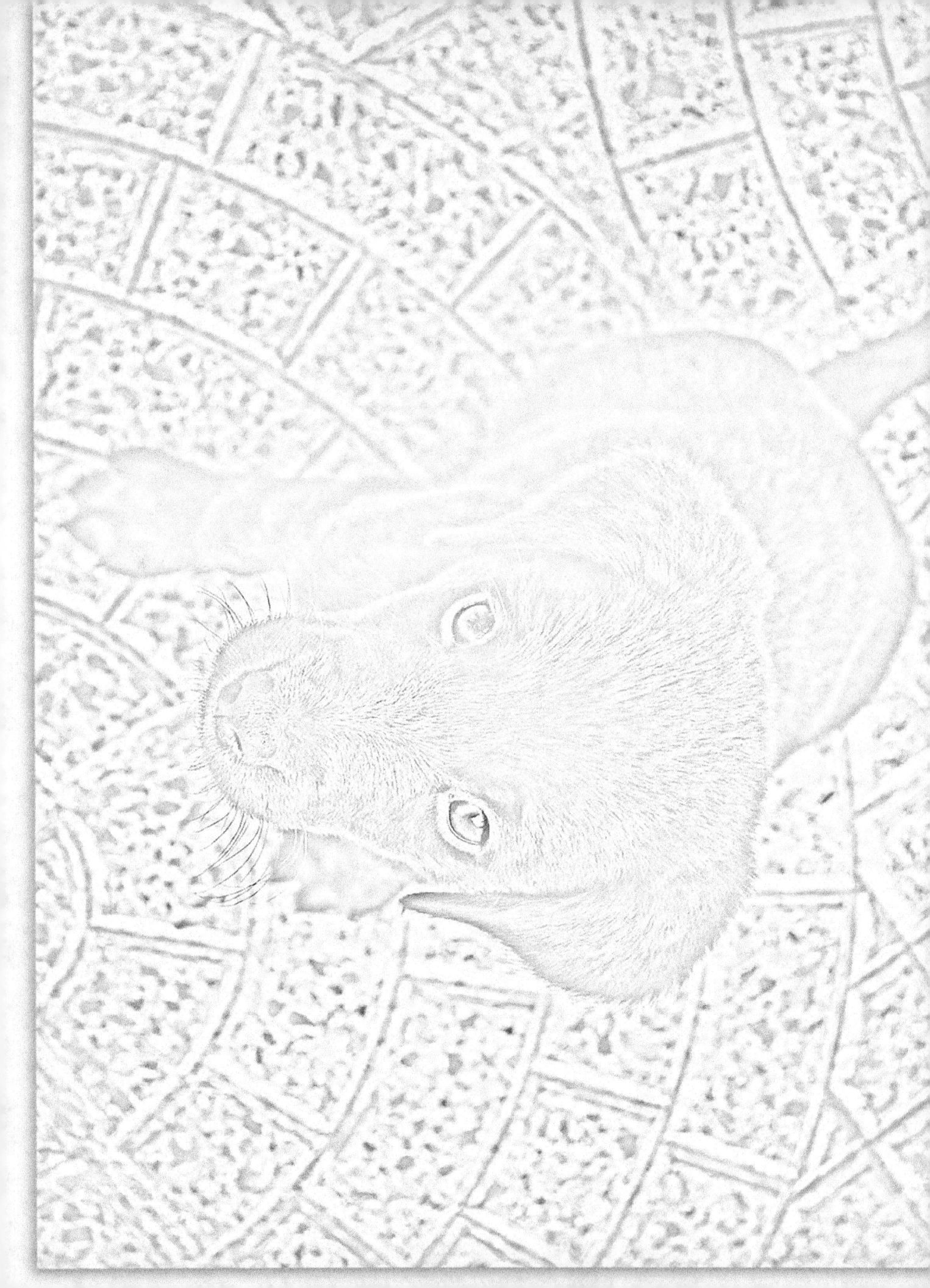

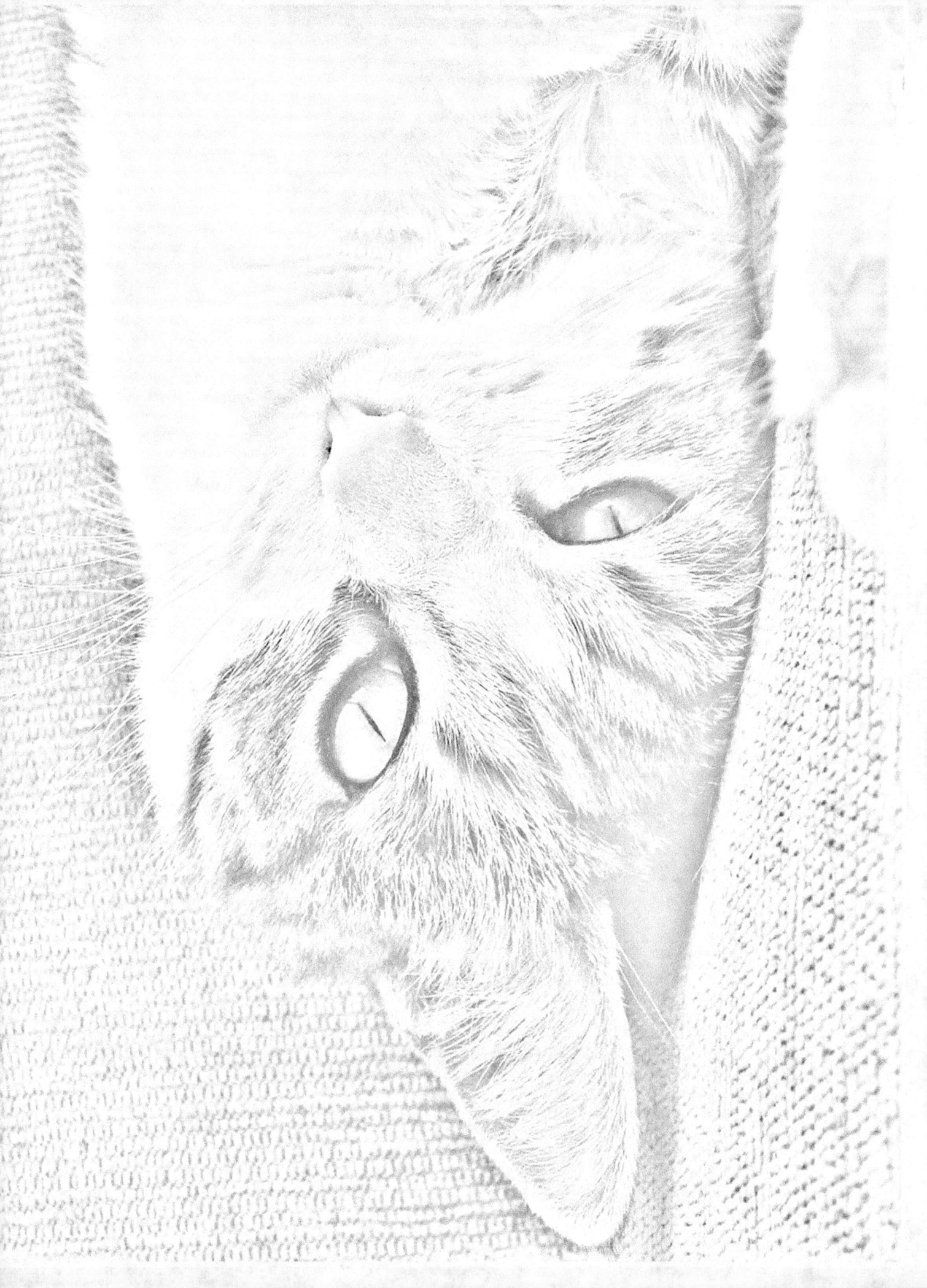

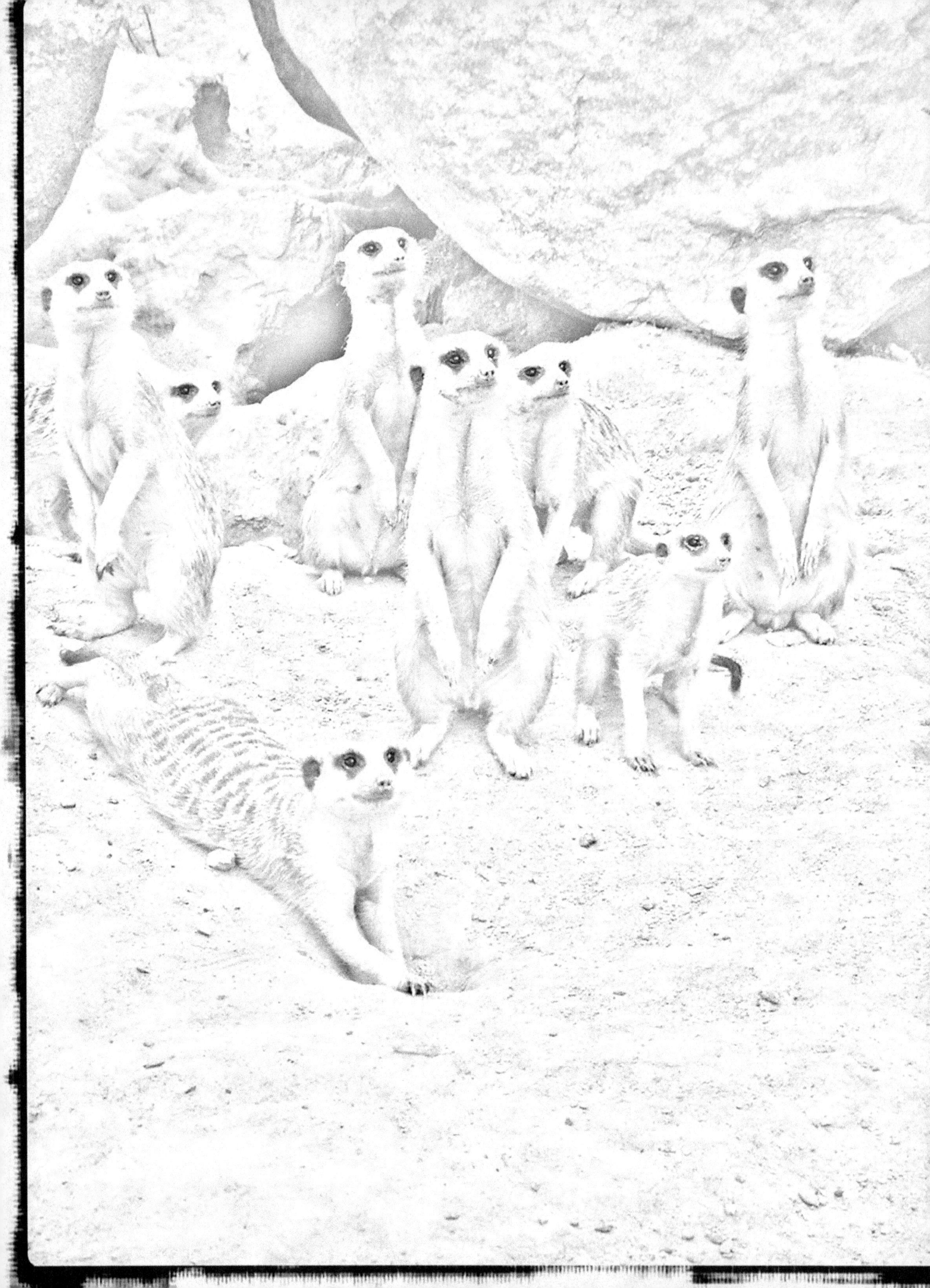

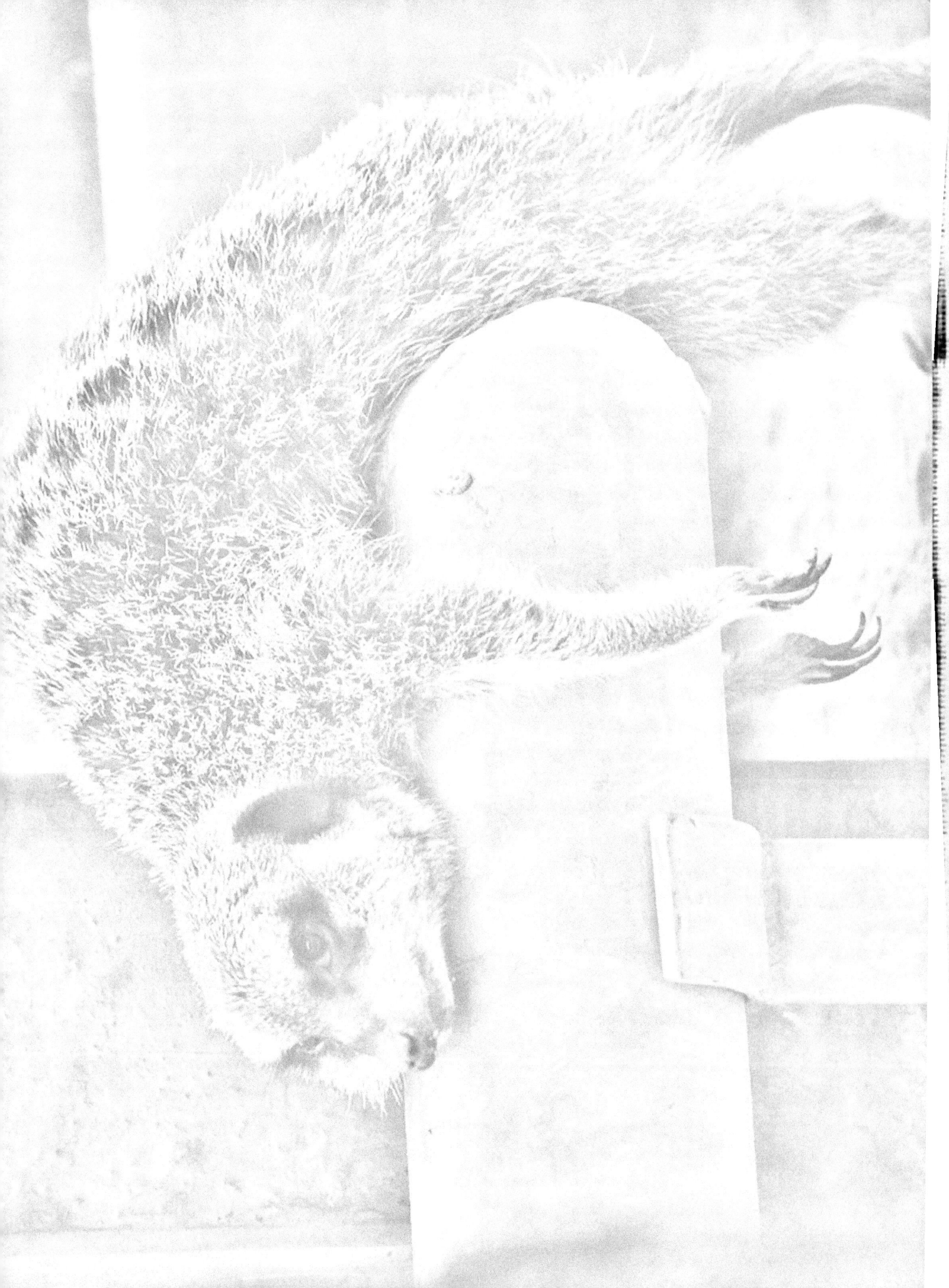

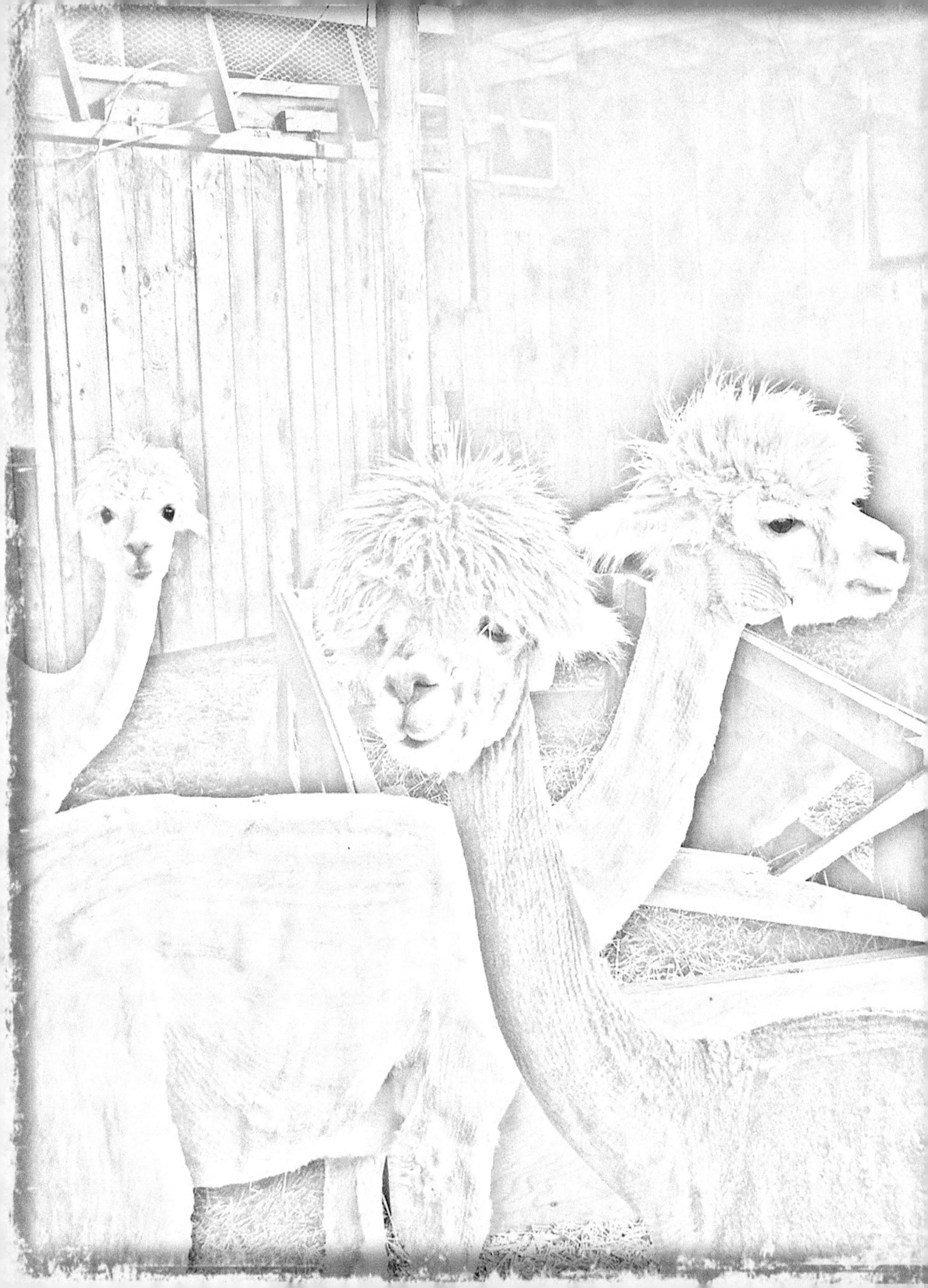

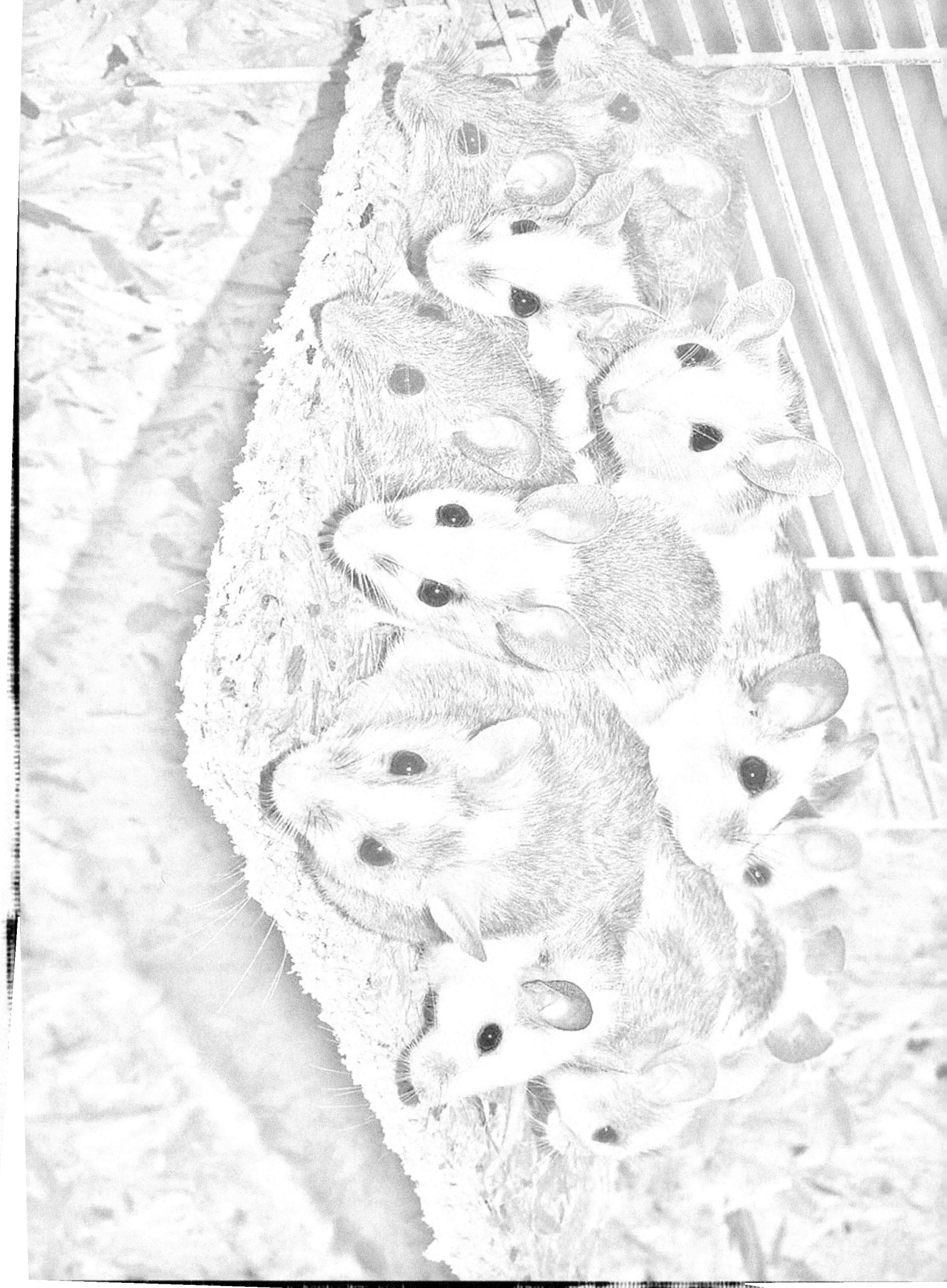

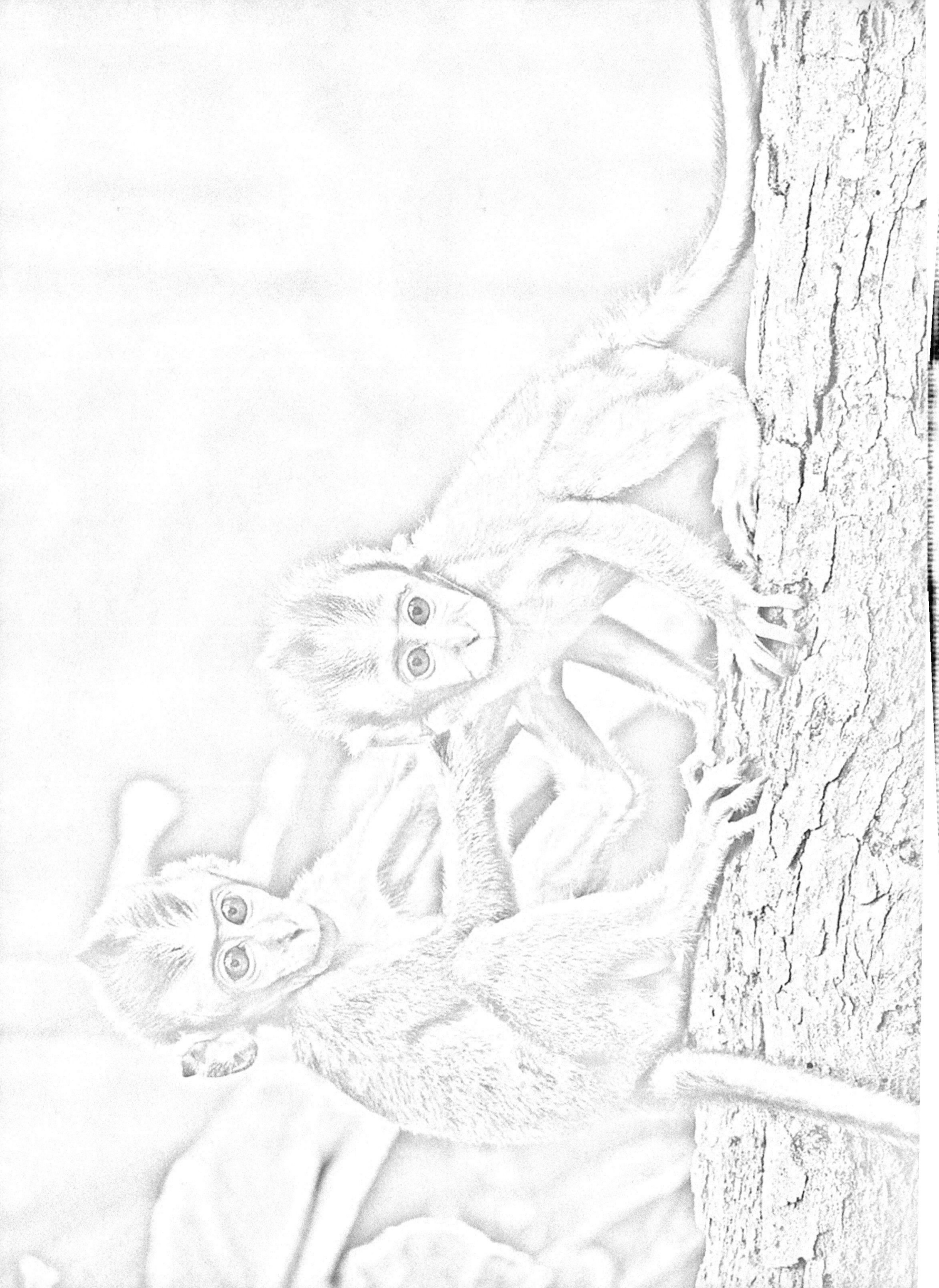

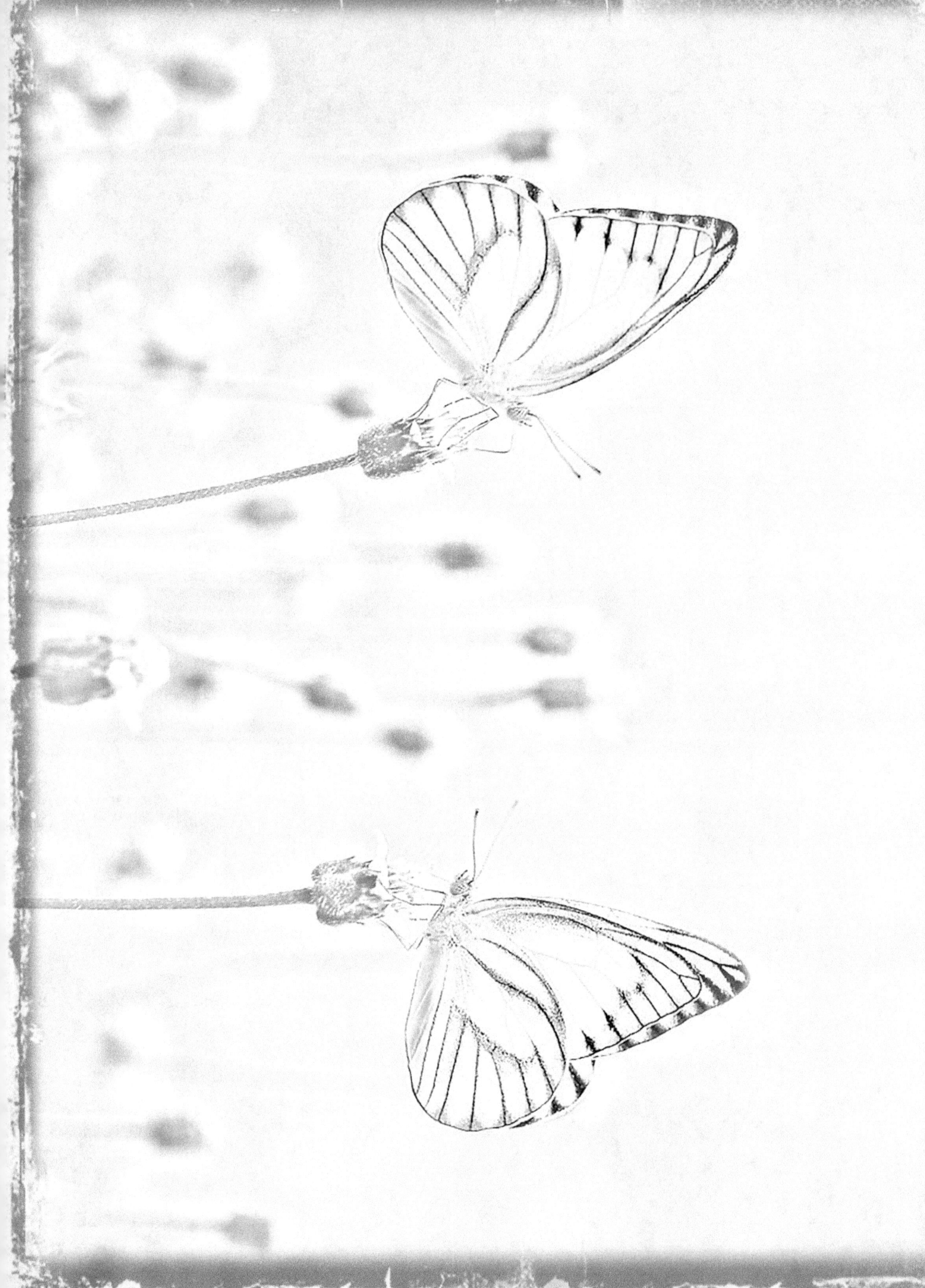

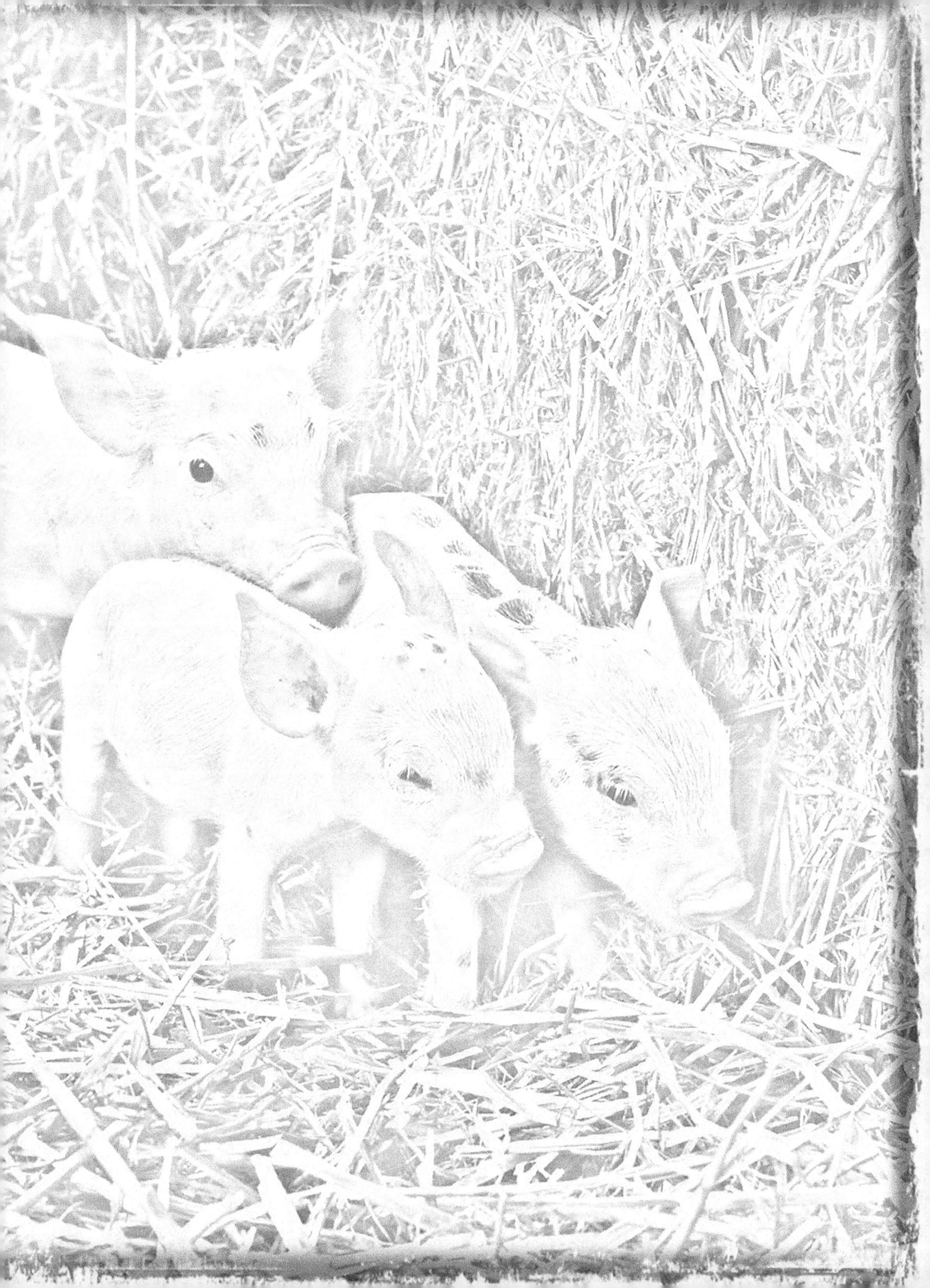

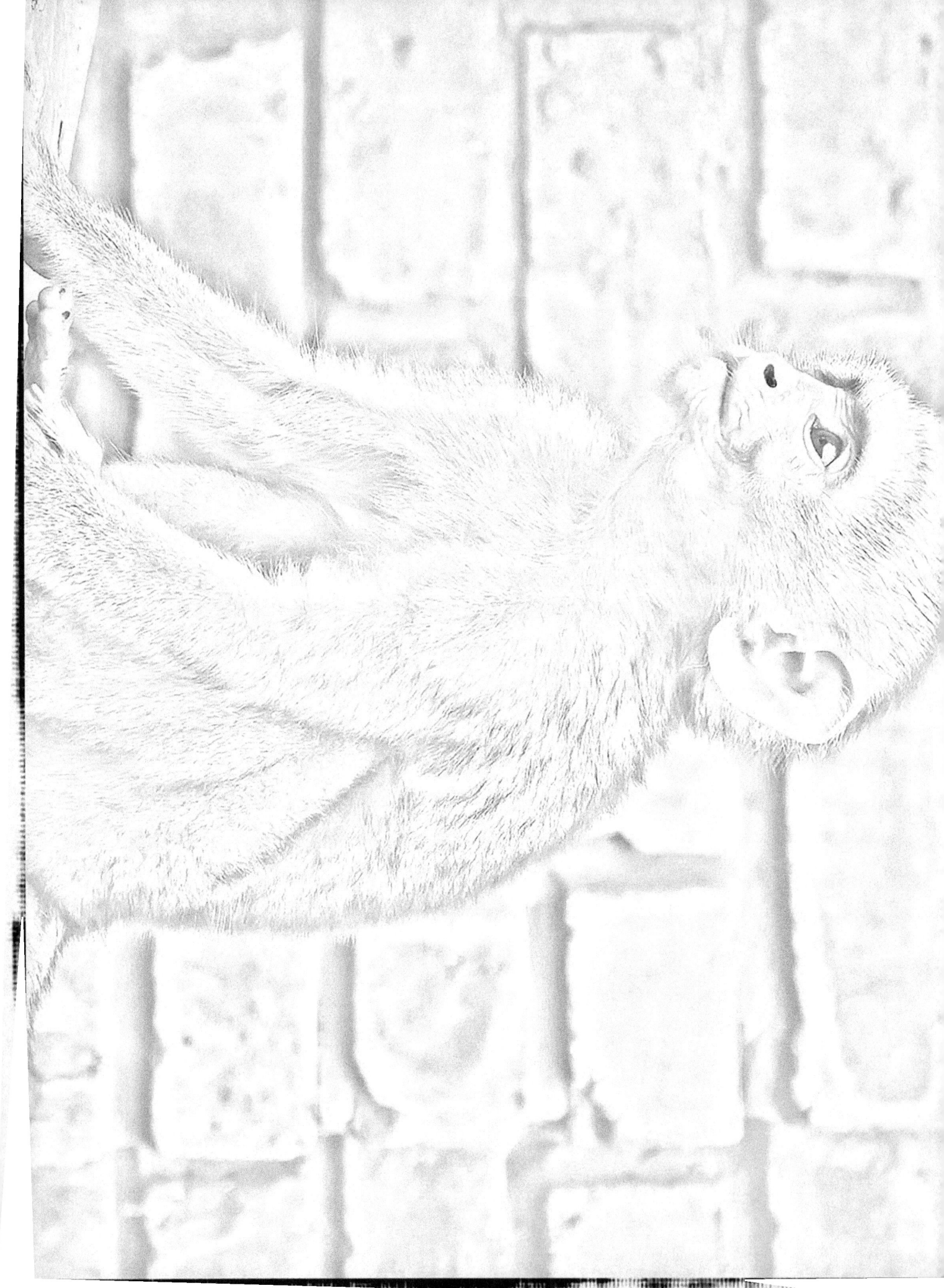

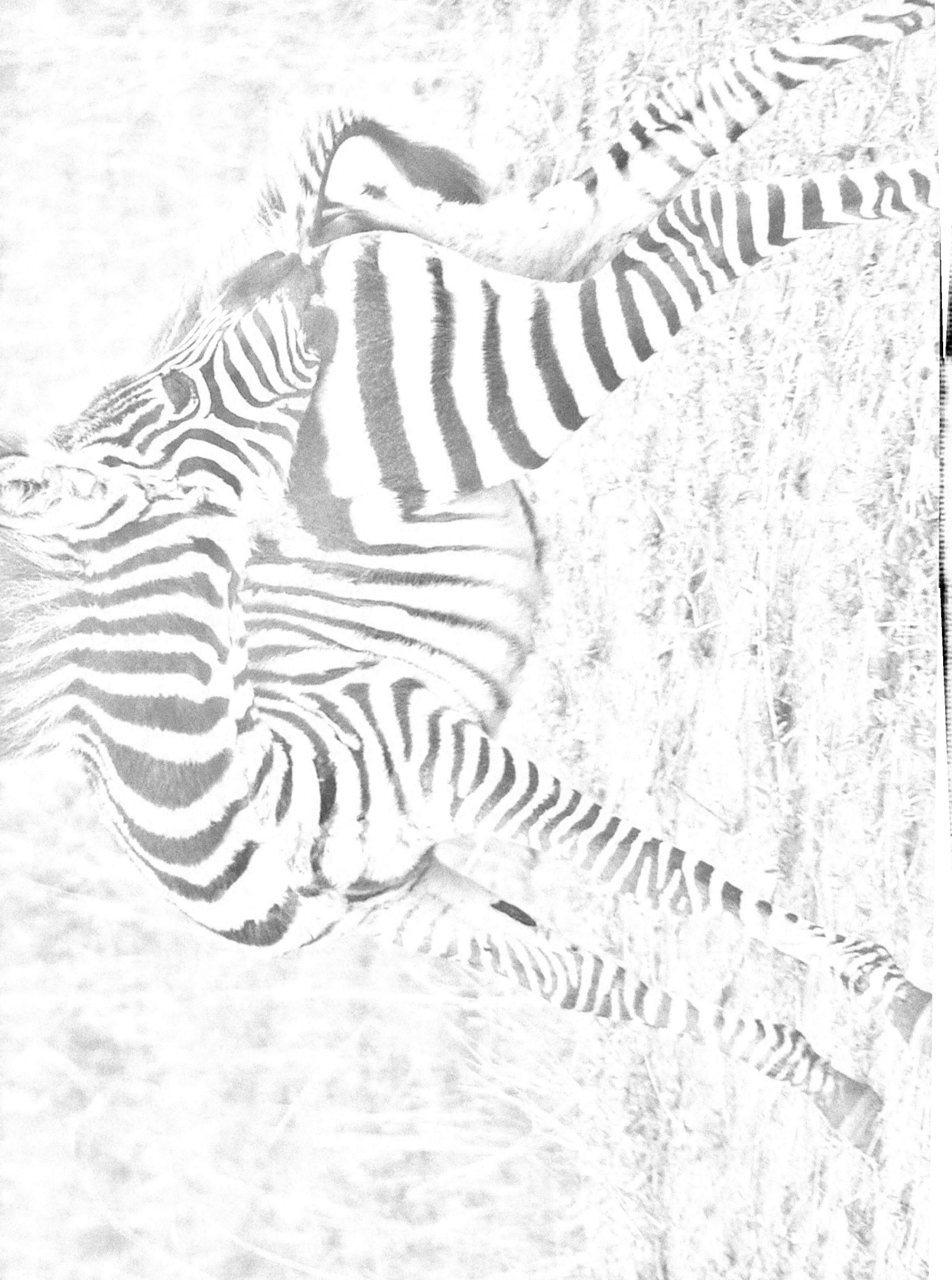

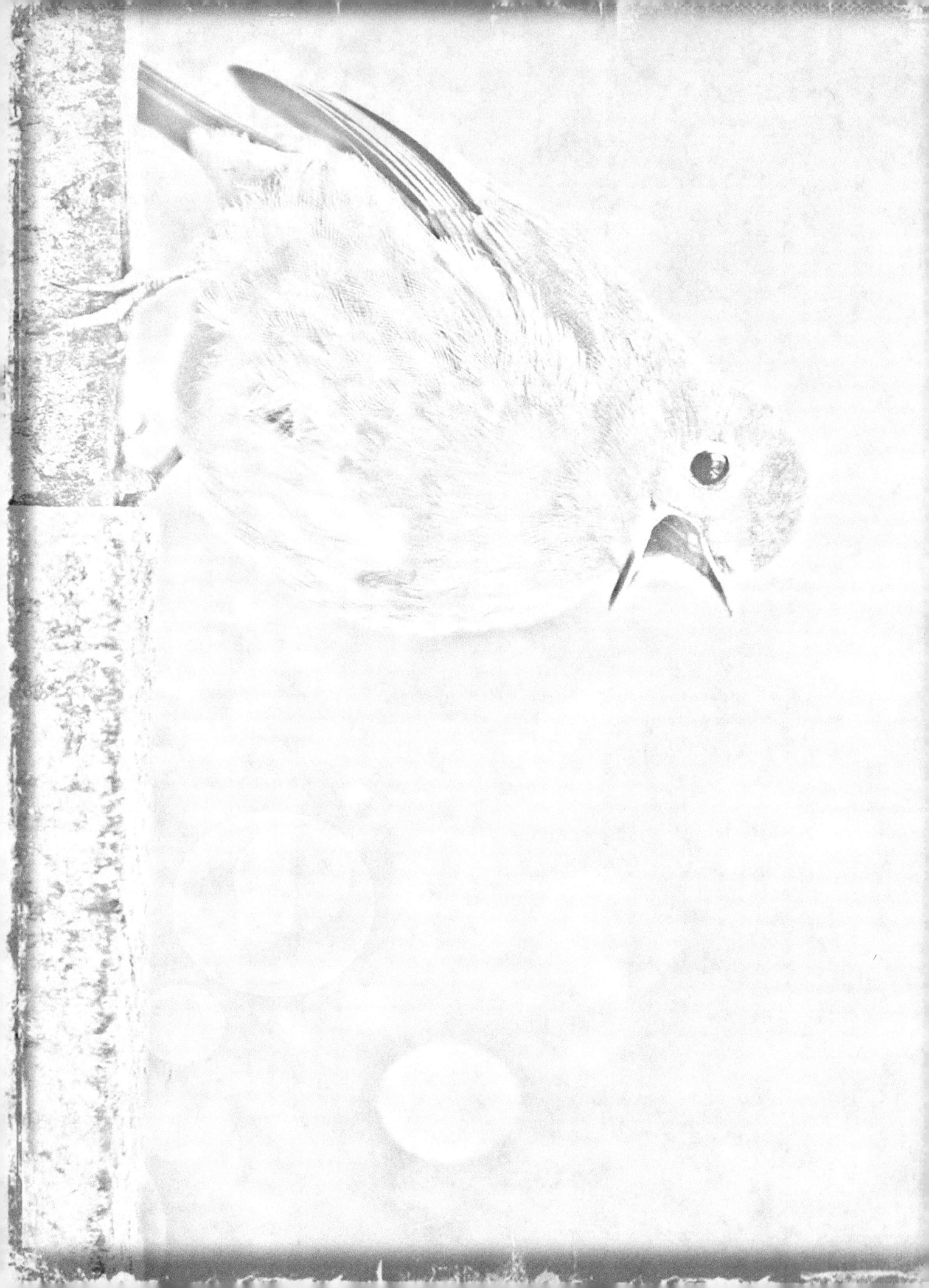

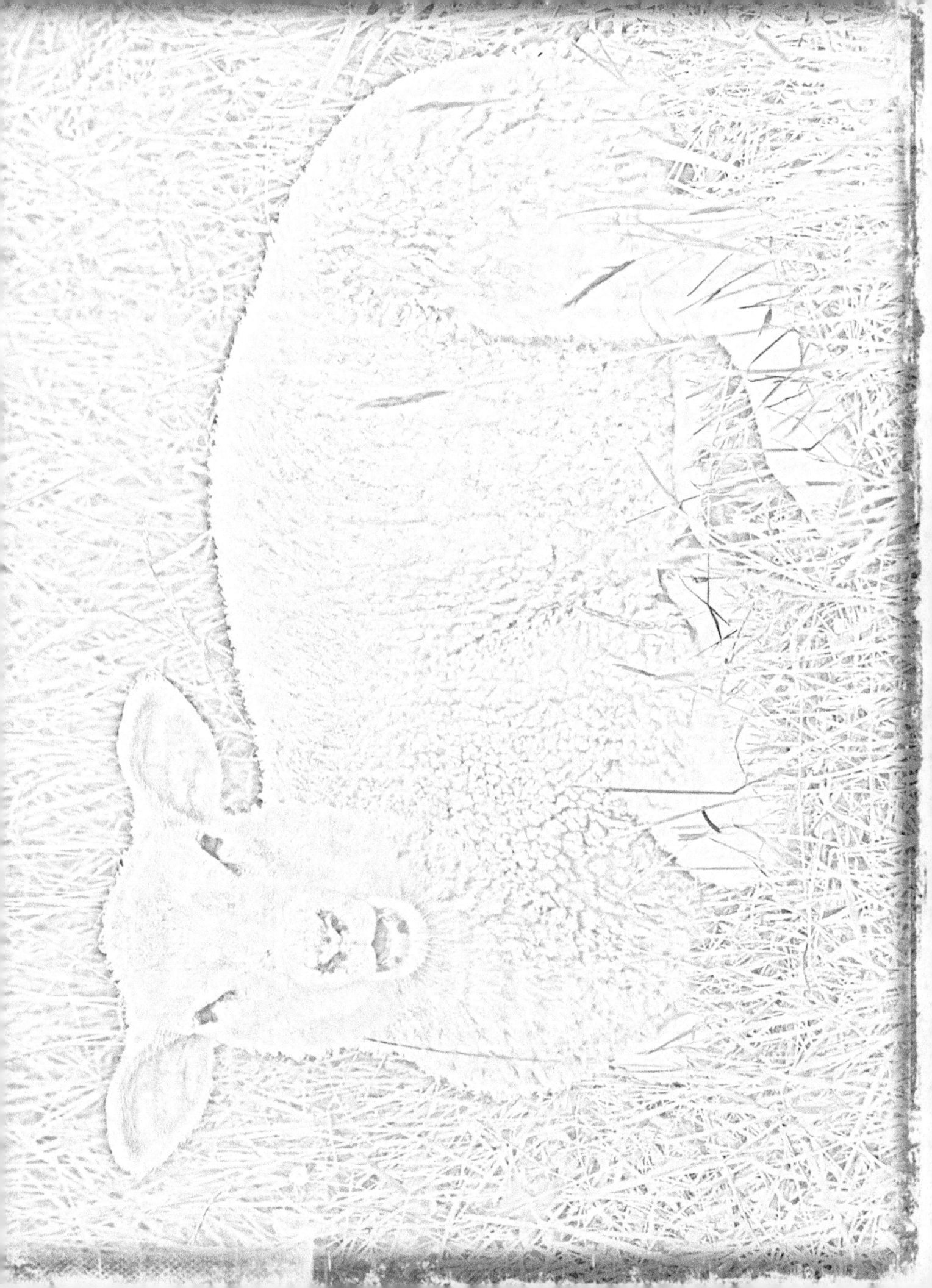

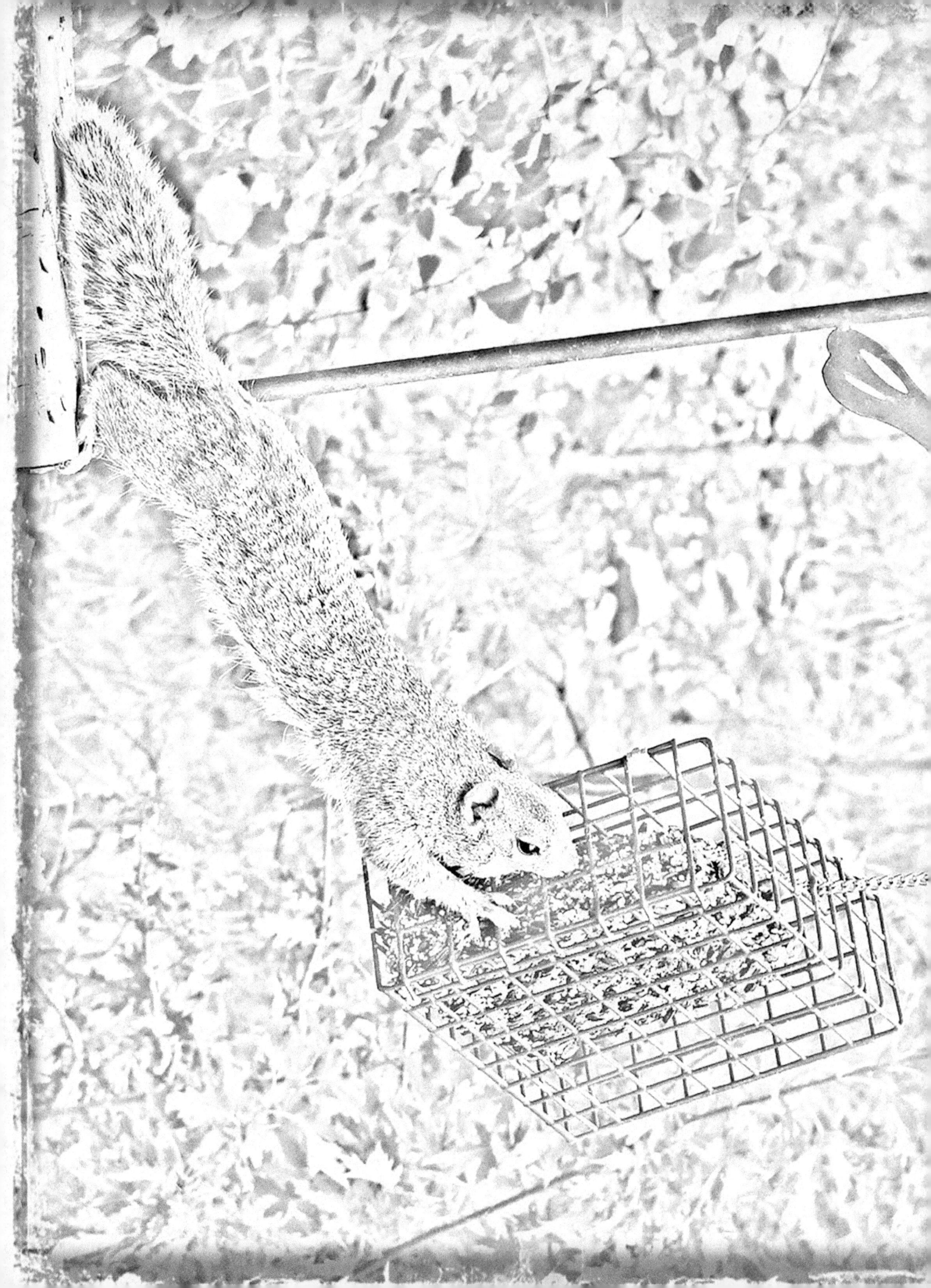

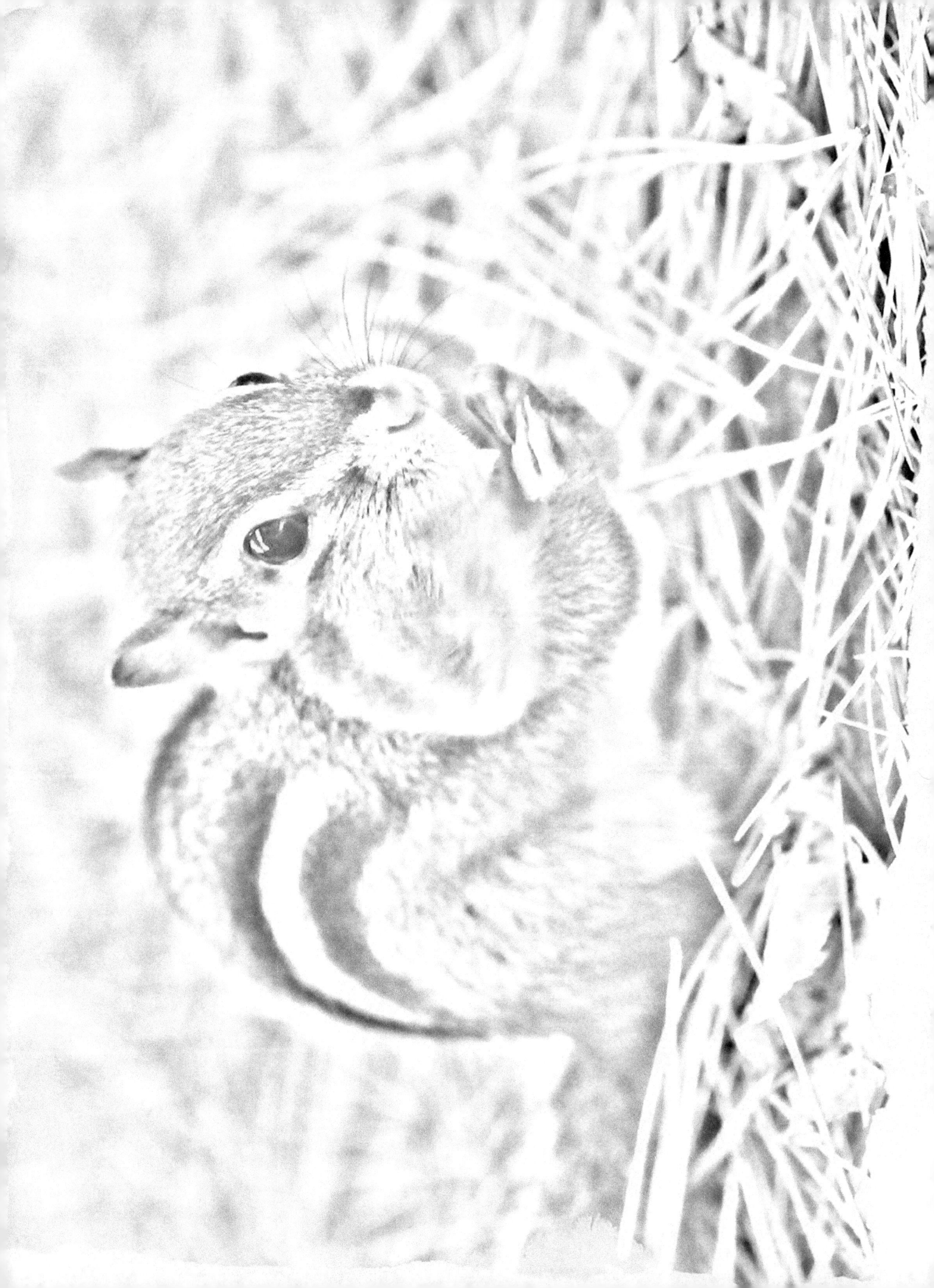

www.ingramcontent.com/pod-product-compliance
Lightning Source LLC
Chambersburg PA
CBHW080524190526
45169CB00008B/3045

9781532744532